Praise for *Blossoms of Friendship*

Vimala Thakar's *Blossoms of Friendship* is an extraordinary roadmap of the mind that will be of interest to anyone who is serious about the practice of meditation. With the precision of a physicist, Thakar reveals the distinct layers of the mind in a refreshingly original yet accessible manner. Through these talks, she firmly places herself in the league of iconoclastic spiritual teachers, such as the late Krishnamurti.

—Donna Farhi, author of *Bringing Yoga to Life:*
The Everyday Practice of Enlightened Living and *Yoga Mind, Body*
and Spirit: A Return to Wholeness

Blossoms of Friendship captures the timelessness of Vimala Thakar's discourses and presents each one as a savory treat. My favorite is Chapter Five, "The Silence of Meditation," which clearly reminds us of the power, even the necessity, of spiritual practice in today's world.

—Judith Lasater, Ph.D., P.T., author of *Living Your Yoga:*
Finding the Spiritual in Everyday Life
and *Relax and Renew: Restful Yoga for Stressful Times*

Blossoms of Friendship

blossoms
of friendship

YOGA WISDOM CLASSICS ■

Vimala Thakar

Rodmell Press
Berkeley, California 2003
First North American Paperback Edition

First Edition published by Motilal Banarsidass, Delhi, India, 1973

Printed in the United States of America
07 06 05 04 03   1 2 3 4 5
ISBN 1-930485-02-6

Library of Congress Cataloging-in-Publication Data

Thakar, Vimala.
  Blossoms of friendship / Vimala Thakar.-- 1st North American
Pbk. ed.
      p. cm. — (Yoga wisdom classics)
  ISBN 1-930485-02-6 (pbk. : alk. paper)
  1. Spiritual life—Hinduism. I. Title. II. Series.
  BL1237.32.T43 2003
  294.5'436—dc21
                                                    2003003701

Editor	Donald Moyer
Copy Editor	Katherine L. Kaiser
Production Editor	Linda Cogozzo
Indexer	Ty Koontz
Cover and Book Design	Gopa & Ted2, Inc.
Author Photograph	Courtesy of *What Is Enlightenment?*
Lithographers	McNaughton & Gunn, Inc.

Text set in Bembo

Contents

Foreword

Rodmell Press is proud to launch the Yoga Wisdom Classics series with this first North American edition of *Blossoms of Friendship* by Vimala Thakar. Although she gave these talks at Mount Abu, India, in 1973, they are as relevant to our lives today as when they were first delivered. Vimala reminds us about the true source of our yoga practice by engaging us in the spirit of inquiry.

Vimala was born in India in 1922, the daughter of a Brahmin family. Her spiritual inquiry began at the tender age of five. From her early years, her father, a lawyer and a confirmed rationalist, allowed her to visit ashrams and spiritual teachers, but encouraged her never to surrender her inner authority to another being.

Vimala's grandfather was a friend of Swami Vivekananda (1863–1902), who introduced yoga philosophy to the United States, in 1893, at the Parliament of Religions in Chicago. Following the death, in 1886, of his teacher, Ramakrishna, Vivekananda went on a pilgrimage across India, and was deeply disturbed by the severe poverty and malaise that he encountered. He devoted himself to a reinterpretation of Vedanta that emphasized not withdrawal from the world, but active social involvement. He supported the emancipation of women and the weakening of the caste system. He founded Ramakrishna Mission centers throughout India, which were dedicated to meditation and social and educational services.

In the tradition of Vivekananda, Vimala is both a spiritual inquirer and a social reformer. As a young woman, she became involved with the Land Gift Movement of Vinoba Bhave, a friend and colleague of Mahatma Gandhi. For a number of years, Vimala traveled around India and gave public talks about the Land Gift Movement, persuading wealthy landowners to donate parcels of land to their poorer tenants.

In 1956, during one of her tours, Vimala was invited to attend a series of talks by J. Krishnamurti (1895–1986), author of *Freedom from the Known*.

These talks, and her subsequent private interviews with Krishnamurti, were to bring about a profound transformation of her life.

Born into a Brahmin family near Madras, Krishnamurti was discovered at the age of twelve by Annie Besant and C. W. Leadbeater, leaders of the Theosophical Society, who took him from his family and raised him to become the next World Teacher. However, a series of nerve-shattering psychophysical experiences led Krishnamurti to reject organized religion and conditioned ways of thought, and in 1929 he renounced the role of World Teacher and left the Theosophical Society. For the next fifty years, he lectured and dialogued in the United States, Europe, and India. He was a renowned spiritual teacher who paradoxically warned against spiritual dependence on teachers and advocated the cultivation of awareness and self-knowledge.

In *On an Eternal Voyage* (1966), Vimala writes about her meetings and interviews with Krishnamurti in the period 1956–1961. Her connection with him went beyond the intellectual and spiritual realms to a deep psychic level. In 1959, Vimala suffered from intense pain and bleeding in her ears, accompanied by high fevers. Feeling herself close to death after an unsuccessful operation, she agreed to journey to England for treatment. Before her departure, Krishnamurti confided that he had healing powers and offered to help her. With his first laying on of hands, the bleeding stopped and her pain was eased. With a few more sessions she was completely healed.

These events precipitated a great change in her consciousness, and she decided to leave the Land Gift Movement. When Vimala met Krishnamurti again in December 1961, he encouraged her to devote her life to the task of dispelling ignorance and cultivating self-knowledge. He said, "Go, shout from the housetops, 'You are on the wrong track! This is not the way to peace.'" From that time until 1991, Vimala traveled throughout India, Europe, and the United States, giving talks and leading retreats. She now lives for much of the time in silence at her home in Mount Abu, India, and prefers leading meditation retreats to giving talks.

In 1983, I had the privilege of attending a weekend conference with Vimala at the Unitarian–Universalist Church of Berkeley, in Kensington, California. Twenty years later, I can still feel her physical presence: quiet, respectful, and nurturing. During discussion periods in particular, I remember how she listened not just with her mind, but with her whole being, sometimes closing her eyes for a few moments, as though physically assimilating the question. When asked about the assassination of Martin Luther King Jr., an associate of hers in the peace movement of the 1960s, a sudden violent tremor passed through her body before she returned to calm.

Vimala was more concerned with the nature of the question than with her answer. She was infinitely patient in helping each participant discover the question that he or she really wanted to ask: the question behind the question. As a result of the caring and trusting environment she created, people asked the most wonderful questions! When Vimala responded, she did not put forward her own opinion, but explored the situation step-by-step from the questioner's point of view. Her method of discourse was a unique combination of clarity and compassion.

The talks collected in *Blossoms of Friendship* are motivated by the same spirit of inquiry: they show clarity of thought and purity of purpose. Although the influence of Krishnamurti on Vimala's teaching method is obvious, the depth of her knowledge and understanding of the yoga tradition is not so apparent. Vimala may not mention Patanjali's Yoga Sutras by name, but her insights into the states of attention, awareness, and meditation provide a clear exegesis of the last three stages of the eightfold yogic path: *dharana, dhyana,* and *samadhi.* For yoga students who want to deepen their understanding of Patanjali's Yoga Sutras, these talks will be especially welcome.

Donald Moyer, Publisher
Rodmell Press
Berkeley, California
January 2003

CHAPTER ONE

Concentration, Attention, and Awareness

Mount Abu; July 12, 1973

Let us begin our inquiry by considering concentration, attention, and awareness. Concentration is attention that is limited by motive, by direction, and by time duration. Motive gives direction and thereby creates the boundaries of attention. Concentration is attention that has chains on its hands and feet as it were.

You can have a motive in relation to known things: things that are known to you, to your family, to your community, to your fellow countrymen, or to the human race at large. You can have a motive in relation to things that have been experienced by people all over the world. But a motive in relation to the unknown is impossible. You can have a motive in relation only to that which has been known, experienced, measured, evaluated, and judged, either by you or by your family or community, and so on, and so on. That is how we have been brought up.

Now, divinity (call it divinity, call it God, call it reality, call it the universal intelligence, call it cosmic consciousness, call it the totality of existence: give it any name) is not in the category of the known, the experienced, the compared, the evaluated, and the judged. The human race has inhabited the globe for millions of years, but there are things that have not been adequately verbalized yet, like truth, beauty, love, and freedom. And silence has not yet been measured. It has not been grasped by the mind and put into the framework of time and space. So in relation to the known, there can be motives. Concentration is an activity always in relation to the known. Either you want it or you want to give it up.

There is another kind of mental activity that is called attention. Attention is the involuntary reflex action of the brain, of the cerebral organ. When your eyes are open, they see things. You may not look at things, but the involuntary action of the eyes is to see objects; the involuntary action of the ears is to hear sounds; the involuntary action of the nose is to smell odors, scents, perfumes, fragrances. The involuntary action, the action built into the very structure of the skin, is to feel the touch, the hot, the cold, the pleasant, and the unpleasant. In the same way, the human brain has been made sensitive in such a way that its built-in action is to attend to things, even without a motive.

Concentration, which is based upon motive, gives direction and limits attention. Attention is an involuntary cerebral activity. You can't change it, you can't suppress it, you can't inhibit it, unless you use violence against yourself. You use violence in many forms. Either you dull the brain with medicines, with drugs, or you dull the brain by repetition of certain words, chanting them over and over again so that the brain moves in a channel and can't move outside of the channel. It is the built-in action of the brain to attend to things. Your eyes are closed and there is a bird chirping somewhere on some branch of some tree and the brain attends to it. Being a cultured and civilized human being, your brain immediately distinguishes the sound of the horn of a car from the sound of the call of a bird: it says, *That is the horn of a car.* A person who has lived in deep jungles or forests somewhere in Africa or in Australia will not be able to recognize the noise of the jet plane flying over a city. It may not be possible for the person living in a village to distinguish the sound of a transistor, a tape recorder, a radio, and so on. So civilization has developed certain powers, cultivated certain powers, and now they are built into your brain and my brain. That is our inheritance. The cultivated brain is our inheritance, and people living in countries where science and technology have advanced to a very considerable extent have very sophisticated brains.

So the brain attends to a sound. And what does "attending to" imply? Recognizing. First, cognition: there is a sound. The brain cognizes. Then recognition: the brain recognizes, that is to say, it identifies and gives the sound a name, distinguishing it from others. That is what naming implies. You give a name to distinguish one thing as separate and independent of the other, separate from the other. There is a car passing by, there is a child shrieking, and so on. So attention means cognition, identification, recognition, and naming.

All this goes on and I don't think it is bondage. The naming and the identifying process in the brains of cultured and civilized people is a very harmless, innocent cerebral activity. It goes on. The brain attends to it. It is not concentration. The mind has not come into play to focus all the brain's energy on a certain purpose in order to gain something from it. It is just simple, innocent, bare attention, which is bound to go on as long as you and I are alive. And I think that is the beauty of human life. Attention is different from concentration, and yet it is an activity of the brain.

Now from attention we move to awareness. Awareness is the nature of intelligence. It has nothing to do with the brain, with intellect, with naming, with identifying. So first of all, when one sits down in silence, one plunges into an unconditional relaxation. One comes face-to-face with this deep-rooted habit of concentrating on things. One says, *I am sitting down in silence, but the bird disturbs me.* The bird won't disturb me unless I concentrate upon it. I attend to it and call it a disturbance the moment I judge it, evaluate it, the moment I have concentrated upon it. So I say, *It disturbs me, it distracts me.* The moment I say that it distracts me or it disturbs me, it indicates that I have been resisting.

Resistance is inverted concentration. Resistance as a form of concentration has got to be unmasked. Before one can proceed toward meditation, it is absolutely necessary to unmask various activities. Resistance is a form of concentration: otherwise, why should it disturb me? The fact that it disturbs me implies that I have formed a relationship with it, a relationship of resistance. It is as if the bird is singing in order to disturb me, as if the car is passing by in order to distract me. I relate myself in that way. Resistance implies relationship. A relationship that has the friction of resistance leads to disharmony.

I wish that you could see the beauty of this. Unless you form a relationship of resistance, there cannot be disturbance and distraction. And one speaks this out of personal experience. For the past thirty or forty years that one has lived, one has not come across things and individuals who could disturb, who could distract. To be disturbed or distracted by something means it irritates me, it annoys me. I want to do something, and it does not allow me to do it. You build up a relationship with disturbance or distraction.

When you are attending—that is to say, when the brain is attending—to objects and there is no resistance built up by the mind, due to certain motives, for certain purposes, the attention burns as brightly as a flame. This is again a cerebral activity. This is a habit of the brain to attend to things. In that state of attention, whatever flows is allowed to flow, allowed to come in and move out, allowed to come up from within and subside. Thus in the mirror of attention it becomes possible for you to look at yourself: the feelings, the thoughts, the sentiments, and the emotions. You are looking at yourself. When you stand before the mirror you are looking at yourself. There seems to be the other, and yet there is no other. There is only you yourself and there is the mirror and there is the activity of looking at yourself.

This metaphor is very important for what we are going to talk about. We have to deal with things invisible, intangible, and so we will need the help of metaphors without stretching them too far, without making them ugly. So attention enables you to be in a state where thoughts, experiences, and memories are looked at. Yet you are looking at them, but not concentrating upon them. The moment that you begin to analyze them, you are concentrating upon them. The moment that you compare and evaluate them, you slip from the state of attention into the state of concentration.

It is a slippery ground between attention and concentration. If, for the fun of it, you sit before a mirror and look at your hands, nose, clothes, and the shape of your body, you are looking at particular parts of yourself. The relation is in duality. But you can look at your own body—you see your image, you see your reflection—but you are not looking at particular parts of your body. You are not looking at the clothes, the feet, the hands: it is just seeing and not looking. Then you are aware. When you look at particular parts of the body, you are aware of the shape of the mirror, you are aware of things that are behind you getting reflected into the mirror. You are aware of the light of the sun coming through the window toward the mirror, and of the play of the light and the dance of the light in the mirror and in the room: you are aware of the whole room. The moment that looking at particular parts of the body is over, you are in the state of seeing. Seeing enables you to be aware of yourself, of the reflection, of the mirror, and of the ceiling, do you see? Frontiers are widening, horizons of attention begin to widen.

Concentration is a relationship with the particular, and attention is a relationship with the whole. And then, as before, your seeing goes on widening and widening and you are aware. It is not a cerebral activity any more. As long as you were looking at it, it was a cerebral activity, but later on you see the mirror, the walls, and the reflection. You are not looking at anything. You are just seeing. And the seeing changes into being aware.

Awareness is the nature of intelligence that vibrates in the universe. Awareness is the purest movement of energy. We have talked about the physical, we have talked about the cerebral, and now we come to awareness, which is a movement of intelligence contained in your whole being. When you listen to music, you do not hear only with the ears. First of all, you listen with the ears to the melody, the notes, the volume, the frequency of sound vibrations. Then the listening widens into hearing. You are aware of the notes, the overtones, and the undertones: the whole person is singing. You are aware of the movement of singing in the person and the movement that music has brought about within you. So listening grows into awareness: awareness of the musician, awareness of the listener, awareness of the surroundings. So awareness is a movement of the sensitivity, of the intelligence, that is vibrating in the whole of you. When you are near a forest, mountain, hill, lake, beautiful field, or seashore, your whole being becomes aware of the scenery. Those who look only with the eyes will get bored with the mountains, the river, or the Himalayas in no time. Because they look only through the eyes, and hear only through the ears, they do not allow the looking and listening to grow into awareness. Concentration and attention and then unresisted attention—unmutilated attention—develops into awareness. It is no longer a cerebral activity: it has become the movement of your total sensitivity, of your intelligence, of your whole being. It is a happening in your totality. And yet I say that this is not meditation.

Awareness has a movement, the movement of intelligence, which is the nature of energy outside you and within you. This is not yet meditation. But it leads you to the threshold of the state of meditation. Intelligence is the movement of energy. It is the purest form of movement, not contaminated by the ego, not contaminated by the me, the self; not contaminated by the cerebral structure, the thoughts, the feelings, the sentiments, the habits, the values, or ideologies. It is untouched by the human mind, and yet it is a movement of energy. Tomorrow morning we will see how energy is the property of matter. But even the movement of intelligence, even the state of awareness, is not the state of meditation, because you are still in the field of very subtle matter. Energy and movement go together; energy is the property of matter. Movement is an indication that we are still in the field of matter. We are proceeding very slowly and very gradually, because we are dealing with meditation, which is a new dimension of consciousness. The whole human race is struggling emotionally and intellectually to grow into an entirely new dimension of life. So this is not a game of words; this is not speculation; this is not sentimentalism. This is something that you have to explore within the laboratory of your own mind and body.

From concentration you move to attention. In the state of attention, there are no frontiers; there is no direction; there is no motive; but still there is you looking at yourself, which is a cultivated duality, a conceptual duality. From attention you grow into the state of awareness, where there is no "I" and "it," there is no "me" and "you": there is only a movement of intelligence vibrating. The person is living and therefore vibrates with intelligence. That is the sensitivity contained in his or her body. Concentration involves mind, memory, experience, and energy. Every attention involves the habit pattern of the cerebral organ. Awareness implies and involves sensitivity of the totality and yet there is movement. And wherever there is movement, there is energy. Energy is the property of matter, and therefore a person living in the state of awareness of the totality is not yet in the state of meditation.

Those of you who have been with me in Norway, the Netherlands, or California know very well that I am interested in this subject from an educational point of view, that is, the education of the human psyche, the human race trying to educate itself and grow into a new dimension. So I deal with meditation as far as words can carry us rationally, scientifically, and sanely. As long as the brain can work, we have to move with the brain. If you deny the brain, then there will be an inhibition and every inhibition is an intrusion and is an obstruction. If you go against the brain, if you deny the brain, if you deny yourself, or if you deny sentiments, the emotions, then every suppression will lead to a psychosomatic obstacle. So we are not going to do that. We will go with reason as far as it takes us. This helps the inquirer to maintain his freedom, his initiative, and his balance of mind.

If you surrender your freedom and expect everything to be done for you by others, then you give up your initiative and you give up the balance of your mind. Man has struggled for freedom in the political and economic field. He should be careful not to throw away his psychic freedom. There will be exchanges, there will be communications, there will be discussions with persons who have made the inner journey, but the exchanges will be in the atmosphere of friendship and not in the atmosphere of authority. Man has struggled for freedom for so many centuries: witness the American Revolution, the French Revolution, the Bolshevik Revolution, the Indian Revolution under Gandhi, the Negroes struggling for freedom under the guidance of Martin Luther King Jr., the Africans struggling under the leadership of Kenneth Kaunda and Jomo Kenyatta. So if you value economic, political, and social freedom, don't give up your psychic freedom in a minute in exchange for a few shabby experiences. Those who say that without the relationship of authority, spiritual exploration cannot take place, are doing damage to the human mind. I say to you, it is possible. It has been possible. If it has been possible in the life of an average person—Vimala, who sits before you—then it can happen in your own life. It can happen provided there is an inquiry, provided the inquiry is correlated with your whole life, and provided the inquiry is allowed to grow, blossom, and bring about changes in your life.

This is something very serious that I am communicating every day. Bit by bit, step by step, we will go into the deeper regions of the human psyche.

CHAPTER TWO

The Movement of the Mind

Mount Abu; July 13, 1973

The brain, or the mind, is a sense organ like any other sense organ in the human body. And thinking, feeling, or willing, or, for that matter, any and every cerebral activity, is a sensual activity. This sense organ, the cerebral structure, is invisible; it is invisible but not intangible; it can be touched and felt through machines maneuvered by man. Thus thinking is as much a material activity or physical activity as any other known and identified physical activity. Just as you hear the sound of cars or perceive objects with the eyes and the optical nerves, and you call it audition or perception, in the same way the brain responds to the challenges and the situations that emerge in daily life. That response is called thinking, feeling, or sentiment, according to its functional nature.

There is movement in the cerebral organ when you think or feel, when you experience emotions or sentiments. When you remember, recollect, contemplate, ponder, or think, there is a very subtle cerebral movement that spreads all over the body and affects the nervous system of the whole being. It affects the chemical condition of the whole being. It is a movement. It is an activity. It consumes energy. It stimulates energy. So in concentration or in the state of attention or observation, a very subtle kind of movement goes on. It is not meditation. The state of experiencing is not the state of meditation; the state of thinking or feeling is not the state of meditation, and in the same way, the state of observation or the state of bare, simple attention is still not the state of meditation.

We saw yesterday that movement indicates energy and energy is the property of matter. Energy exists in matter. If you analyze matter into atoms, electrons, and molecules, you will find that there is energy contained in the finest particle of matter. It is impossible to come across a particle of matter that has no energy and therefore no movement. Matter has energy and energy has movement. Thought is matter. Thinking is a material, sensual activity and has tremendous energy. It has a movement that has been measured by man, qualified, modified, sophisticated, regulated, and controlled by man. Culture and civilization regulate and control cerebral activity and, indirectly, psychophysical and physical activity. They regulate and control psychological and biological movement. The content of culture and civilization is to give cerebral activity a direction, to regulate it, to modify it, to sophisticate it, and so on, and so on. Thus in the state of attention, the brain is moving. The built-in movement of cognition goes on. As the eyes involuntarily see and the ears involuntarily hear, the brain involuntarily is in the state of attention. You may not look at an object, you may only see it, and yet your brain registers the form, the shape, the color, and tells you the name of the object according to your education, culture, and civilization. An Indian villager, for example, will not know what to call a spacecraft or spaceship. He will see a form in the sky. So the brain of a simple villager in India will register the shape, the color, perhaps the material of the spacecraft, but not the name. The villager has not had the education or the cultural upbringing. He does not know the thing. But still the brain registers the color, the shape, the size, the mass, the volume.

If a person does not know Indian music, he will not be able to tell you the raga, the melody, the tila, the time beats, and so on. The person will feel only the volume and perhaps the pitch, if he has the sensitivity. So the registration, the naming, the cognition by the brain take place according to the person's education, culture, or the context of his life: urban life or agrarian life. But it is an involuntary activity of the brain. So the brain is in the state of attention, and whether you want it to or not, it identifies the shape, the size, the color, and perhaps the name. In other words, it is a response of the brain to the movement of life outside the skin. You don't make an effort, but yet there is a movement, movement of the energy contained in the brain.

I am trying to share with you something that I have seen. We have been going step by step for the past couple of days into this very complex and subtle region of the human psyche. The brain indicates the color, the shape, the size, and even the name, but the sting of reaction, that is to say, the activity of the ego, the self, the me, does not take place. The distinction between concentration and attention has to be understood and grasped very clearly. In a state of concentration, you react. You resist. But in a state of attention there is no resistance. There is no analysis. There is no reaction of the ego.

In experiencing, the reactions are very gross and understandable by anyone. In concentration, the reactions are subtle, but still noticeable. In attention, there is no reaction, but movement is still there. When a human being sustains the state of attention and the intensity thereof for some time, intelligence begins to unfold itself. Just as out of a bud the flower blossoms and unfolds itself, so, too, out of unconditional relaxation (the state of attention that is the involuntary cerebral activity through which one has to go), intelligence begins to unfold itself. Intelligence is the sensitivity of the whole body. Attention is a cerebral activity. Concentration includes psychological reaction in addition to cerebral activity. When the attention is sustained, the sensitivity of the whole body begins to unfold itself, to operate and function, so that there is no longer a cerebral activity, but the total existence becomes eloquent.

Awareness is the existential eloquence of the person, and yet the sensitivity, the intelligence expressing itself in awareness, is not meditation. I am aware of the things around me; I am aware of the stillness of my body; I am aware of the state of attention contained in me; I am aware of the vibrations outside and inside me. That is to say, the I, or the state of awareness, and the surroundings, or the life of which I am aware, are distinctly different from each other. In the state of attention, the brain is active; now the whole being acts and yet there is a distinction. I am aware of the totality, but even then I stand outside the totality to be aware of it.

You may be a witness to the whole universe. It indicates that you are trying to stand outside the universe to be aware of it. Thus awareness is still an individual movement: the individual stands apart from the universe; the individual stands apart from the cosmos. That movement of the individual may be in harmony with the universal movement, and it may be in harmony with the cosmic movement, but there is still movement taking place within the individual. The complex consciousness that man has enables him to be aware that he is in the state of awareness. In awareness, you feel the presence of the life around you; you feel the presence of the life within you. You feel the presence not of specific objects that you would count, compare, and evaluate, but you feel the presence of the totality within you and the totality outside you. You feel the coexistence of the individual totality, that is to say, the universe condensed in the human form; after all, that is what you are. So one is aware of the totality contained in the human form existing side by side with the totality outside the skin.

We are now in the region of what is most difficult to verbalize. When you say *I am in the state of awareness,* there is no attention or observation. They are left behind. Even in the state of awareness, it seems to me, movement is taking place in the individual. And movement, indicating energy contained in certain forms of matter, is within the field of time and space, and life is much vaster than time and space. Time and space are contained in life. Movement takes place within time and space. But life also exists outside time and space. The is-ness, the to-be-ness of life, has no movement in it. So human consciousness can take you from the field of experiencing, doing, concentrating, observing, and paying attention, to the state of awareness. The human consciousness, or psyche, can carry you up to the region of awareness. Beyond the state of awareness, there is no consciousness, no movement, no time and space. Perhaps that is the state that could be called the state of meditation, the state of *samadhi.* In meditation, there is no movement. Life has no movement: it is only matter that has movement. Movement and energy are the property of matter. Life is is-ness without any movement whatsoever. That which remains without movement can be called neither individual nor universal. It has no center and no circumference. Intellectual activity has a center, the me, the self, the ego. Awareness as the activity of the intelligence has the whole human body, the human individual, as the center. Beyond awareness, the individual is not at the center. Nothing moves out of the individual. Nothing emanates or radiates from the person. Just as in the state of observation there is no ego-centered activity, so in the state of awareness, the whole cerebral organ does not function. Beyond awareness, the individual entity and the movements contained in the individual entity are simply not there. I wish that I could verbalize this more fully.

In the state of meditation, the ocean of is-ness is left without a ripple. Even that metaphor is imperfect. If I liken it to vast space, even that metaphor does not satisfy me. Because compared to life, space is gross; compared to life, time is gross. The is-ness, the to-be-ness, the suchness of life is something for which one will have to find words to communicate. Mind you, this talk is not an effort to expound anything. This is only a very friendly sharing of something that one sees and something that one lives. But we will proceed with this tomorrow. We talked about concentration, attention, and awareness yesterday. We might talk about movement, vibration, and vibrationless is-ness tomorrow.

CHAPTER THREE

Consciousness Is Matter

Mount Abu; July 14, 1973

I wonder whether it will be possible for me to communicate through words what I would like to share with you this morning, whether it will be possible for me to communicate it in terms that will make some sense to you. Yet there is an urge to share this unusual approach to meditation.

We saw yesterday that the state of awareness is a state of the whole being in which intelligence functions. Intelligence, being the sensitivity, the uncontaminated movement, of the basic energy contained in the being, is not conditioned by knowledge and experience. Intelligence is neither individual nor collective. Knowledge can be individual as well as collective. There can be individual experiences and collective experiences. Like love, sensitivity, truth, and beauty, intelligence is neither individual nor collective; it is neither personal nor impersonal. Thus it is not conditioned by knowledge and experience. It is unmutilated. It is an undivided whole.

This intelligence begins to operate in the state of awareness. Intelligence is the movement of unconditioned energy, but still it is energy. So in the state of awareness, the movement of unconditioned energy goes on. And there is an intercourse between the movement of awareness in the individual and the movement of intelligence outside the individual in the universe. The cosmic intelligence, the cosmic energy, and the unconditioned energy contained in the individual meet together. There is a kind of consummation. Those energies meet without reservation. There is an unconditional encounter between the intelligence contained in the individual and the intelligence contained in the universe. In other words, the individual unconditioned consciousness and the universal, or cosmic, consciousness meet together, in the state of awareness. They are in a deep embrace as it were. That is what the mystics call the marriage between the individual and the universal. The mystical marriage with the beloved, with God, with the divinity, is what Indians call the marriage between Shiva and Shakti. But still it is the meeting between the unconditioned individual energy and the unconditioned energy outside it.

That is a happening that takes place. In the state of awareness there may not be experiences, but there are happenings. Thus when Jesus of Nazareth came down from the mountain after forty days of solitude, his Apostles could not recognize him. A psychic marriage between the individual and the universal consciousness had taken place. He came down with light shining upon the forehead and speaking in terms indescribably simple and elegant. That very simplicity baffled his followers. He had gone through the happening.

After forty-eight days of fasting and penance under the bodhi tree, Siddhartha Gautama became the Buddha. Something happened within him; something happened in the unconditioned part of his consciousness. Something happened in the sphere of intelligence contained in his being. And that day is still marked in history as the day of Buddha's self-realization, the day of Buddha's nirvana.

After twelve long years of penance and austerity, there took place a happening in the life of Mahavira, the so-called founder of the Jain religion. On the plane of intellect, experiences take place. On the plane of intelligence and awareness, happenings take place: happenings that cannot be interpreted into the language of the known, happenings that cannot be captured in the framework of an ego-centered experience. And yet a happening is a movement that takes place in the psyche of the individual. Self-realization as a happening took place in the Buddha's life. One can say that after such a happening, there was light. There was illumination.

The substratum of intelligence is the intellect. The substratum of awareness and intelligence, the substratum of the unconditioned energy, is the conditioned energy, the passively alert brain. It may be passively alert or it may be in choiceless awareness, but it is there as the substratum. You know, in the conditioned psyche, you have the conscious, the subconscious, and the unconscious. Now these three, after becoming a homogeneous whole, go into abeyance, but they are there. Whatever happens on the level of intelligence or awareness has the whole conditioned psyche as the substratum. Otherwise, verbalization of the happening would be impossible. Memory of the happening would be impossible. So the individual as an entity separate from the universe is there. The unconditioned psyche in the individual and the unconditioned psyche in the universe meet together, on the soil of the conditioned total human psyche, the racially conditioned psyche.

There have been efforts to verbalize such happenings. Like Aurobindo, you may call it the descent of the divine taking place in the individual psyche. You may call it the moment of illumination in the life of Ramakrishna, when the image of the Mother Kali disappeared while he was sitting before it with a sword in his hand, yearning and pining in agony for realization. The sword dropped from his hands and the only description we got from his lips afterward was "There was light, light, and light." So at that moment in the psyche of Ramakrishna, something took place.

There is a ripple. There is a happening. Awareness has a movement of unconditioned energy, and energy is the property of matter. Thus even at that level, whatever takes place is not beyond time and space, though it is unrelated to time and space. It is unrelated to time and space in the sense that it cannot use them to bring about this happening. It may be a very significant event because the individual changes. The union with the universal energy, the cosmic consciousness, transforms the individual in many ways. It brings about great changes in his physical and cerebral quality.

And yet I dare say to you, my friends, that this is not silence. And this is not meditation. It is a very significant, romantic thing that can happen to a human being. Man has indulged enough in this romance with the unconditioned energy, the unknown, the unexperienced, the unnamed. He has indulged in this experience, in the East as well as the West, for thousands of years. It has its own beauty. It has its own grandeur. Sensual experience and psychological ecstasy have altogether different qualities from the happening on the level of intelligence or sensitivity. And yet in a way, they are the movements that take place in the individual as an entity separate from the universe. You will be surprised that I call the conditioned psyche the substratum—the undercurrent—of intelligence, or awareness. Why do I call it this? Because those individuals who have gone through such happenings have tried to verbalize them and have said, "It is immeasurable; it is unknowable." Unless there is a consciousness of the measurableness of a thing, how do you call something immeasurable? People have been trying to describe divinity as that which is unknowable, that which is immeasurable and unnameable; but unless I am conscious of the memory, of the activity of naming, the name and the nameableness, how can I call something unnameable and immeasurable? I hope that you see my point that the substratum of the conditioned psyche recognizes the names and the nameableness; the known and the knowableness; the measures and the measurableness. One is aware of all that. Therefore, man has been trying to say, "God is immeasurable, the divinity is unknowable."

The illusion that there is a dichotomy between the known and the unknown, the measurable and the immeasurable, has been persisting in the human mind for thousands of years. Thus even the state of awareness is not the state of silence. It is a state of quietness, no doubt. It is a state of peacefulness, no doubt. It is a state of the ego, with the whole paraphernalia of knowledge and experience going into abeyance. Yet it is not silence. The state of awareness is a state of passive receptivity for the cosmic consciousness to work upon. It has been called peaceful alertness or choiceless awareness. Krishnaji [Krishnamurti] is the only person in the world today who brings his audiences to the threshold of the known and points out the direction toward the unknown and unknowable; who points out the frontiers of all human measurements and brings his audiences with terrible intensity to the doorstep of the immeasurable.

As long as it is possible to describe something as immeasurable, unknowable, and unnameable, you are within the frontiers of time and space. So it may be unconditioned energy, but still it is energy with very subtle matter around it. It is only when the state of awareness subsides completely, when there is neither an awareness of the universe around you nor an awareness of the intelligence, sensitivity, or unconditioned energy within yourself, that silence as a dimension comes to life. The conditioned human psyche and the unconditioned human psyche both become quiet. If the conditioned psyche is quiet and the unconditioned psyche is in a state of passive alertness and choiceless awareness, happenings are bound to take place. I have nothing against these experiences or happenings. Please do not misunderstand me. But one has to see the facts as they are. Just as visions and experiences are the projections of the subconscious and the unconscious, so happenings are the projections of the cosmic and the universal into the individual. Until the state of meditation is reached, one is not in a new dimension of life.

Meditation is a new dimension of life altogether. There one is entirely free of consciousness, which is energy—a very subtle matter contained in the human brain. It is a very daring thing to say that the whole human psyche is very subtle matter, and yet I say that consciousness, whether conditioned or unconditioned, is matter.

CHAPTER FOUR

Friendship and Freedom

International Youth Talk
Mount Abu; July 16, 1973

Those have attended the morning silence session are aware that we shall be meeting from today onward to the end of this month every alternate day for either discourse or discussions. There are fifteen or twenty of us who have gathered here at Mount Abu to meet in an informal way and communicate with one another in an atmosphere of friendship. To come together in the atmosphere of friendship and not in the atmosphere of authority is a very remarkable thing.

Unless we grasp the implications of friendship and freedom, we will not be able to appreciate what is going to take place here for the next week or two. In friendship, there is no dependency; in friendship, there is no authority. There might be an exchange; there might be guidance, if you like, as there might be some guidance by Gajendraji in relation to yoga exercises and pranayama; there might be some guidance about what is balanced nutrition and the essentials of physical and psychological health. So the guidance that is necessary or unavoidable as a part of education might be there, and it might be very difficult to understand that in such guidance there is no dependency or authority. When you go to a person looking upon him or her as an authority, you take his or her words literally. You get conditioned by the life of the person, the conditioning of the person, and the pattern of his or her behavior, both physical and psychological. Because you look upon that person as an ideal person, as an authority, you go there expecting to copy what he or she is doing, to imitate, to conform to his or her way of living; but in friendship, you don't meet a person in order to copy him or her. You meet, you talk, you discuss, you live together, you learn, and you grow: all that happens in the togetherness of friends. There is a mutuality, there is a reciprocity. Maybe this afternoon I am sitting here; tomorrow morning it will be Gajendraji who sits here and addresses you. It does not make any difference. Or another day, someone else might sit here. It does not give you a feeling that you are going to find some protection, some security, in that process. So friendship stimulates freedom but authority stimulates conformity.

Friendship inspires and enriches the lives of those who come together. I am saying this and spelling it out elaborately because you have come to this land from such a long distance, not for a big camp, not for mere lectures, but just to live with me, to talk to me, and to hear me. So I would like you to know my attitude toward the whole thing. That is why we meet in such a small number, in a homely, informal atmosphere. As I said earlier, it is absolutely necessary to eliminate exploitation in the psychic lives of human beings. As long as you accept authority, there will be exploitation. So here we will come together, and you might listen to me. There is no compulsion. If you like the morning talk, then you might come in the evening; if you don't feel like coming, then you don't come. This is not a formal camp. It is an informal, friendly gathering. I used to call it an education camp, but now even the word "camp" pricks somewhere; I don't know what other English word to use.

We come together only for the joy of togetherness: to learn and to grow. The transformation that might take place, the change that might occur, is the side effect, the by-product. Now, why are we coming together? Why are there so many people? I was in Dalhousie in May and June. There were so many young men and women from different countries of the world living in Dalhousie, renting cottages, coming together, sitting in meditation, concentrating. I was in Manali. There, too, I found young men and women from around the world, from Australia, Hawaii, Burma, Japan, the Middle East, West European countries, and Scandinavian countries. Why? Why is there such an urge in the minds of young people to go to a far-off land, to put up with all the inconveniences? What are they looking for? I am not talking about the negligible minority, perhaps a few hundred, who are only trying to find an escape, but about the thousands who are inquiring, searching, exploring, groping, struggling to find something.

It seems to me that the younger generation is tired of the sensual and psychological pleasures and means of pleasures. They are tired of the affluence for which their forefathers struggled so hard. They are tired of the rationalism and idealism of the nineteenth and twentieth centuries. They are tired of wars, and the bare and harsh city life; they are tired of the speed for which their forefathers struggled: the speed of communication, the speed of physical transportation. They are tired of the cinemas, the television, the radio. The children of the affluent countries are turning their backs on affluence. At the same time, men and women in starvation-stricken countries are dying for affluence: not just comfort, not just provision of their physical needs—their minds are hungry and thirsty for affluence. You who come from the United States, Canada, Scandinavia, and the Netherlands do not know what it means for an Indian young man or woman to have a bicycle, to have a car, to have a refrigerator, let alone a television: it is impossible for them to have these things. To have good clothes, to have good fruit, to have good milk: you have no idea what it means for a young man or woman in India or Pakistan or Ceylon, in Indonesia, or in the Middle East. So they are thirsty and hungry for the best clothes, for the best housing, for the means of physical pleasure and psychological excitement and entertainment. There is a polarity.

Now in the East and the West, one is turning away from something for which the other is struggling. That is how the human race lives. At present, and for the next week or two, I am talking to the children of affluence. By "children," I mean the human beings living in the second half of the twentieth century, not the children of the nineteenth or eighteenth centuries: those centuries that are bygone. So having seen the glamour of sensual pleasure, the pleasure of thoughts, feelings, and sentiments, and the pleasure of science and technology, the children of affluence are asking of themselves and of society, *Is there more to life than having a nice house and a car and a television set and a good job and a bank balance?* A computer can think and work and have a memory: what more is there to a human being? A spacecraft can enable man to land on the moon: is there anything more to the human mind that has created the spacecraft? Has man got something that travels faster than the speed of light, the speed of sound, or the speed of a spaceship?

Can man reach the moon without a spaceship? Can man transcend time, which he has created? Can man transcend space? These are the pressures that are troubling and torturing man and woman in affluent countries: *What is beyond time? What is beyond space? What is beyond the brain? What is beyond the mind?* The problems that appear absolutely academic to the Indian mind have become problems of life and death, problems of survival, for young people in Europe, the United States, Australia, and so on.

So it seems that the young men and women who are in revolt against the present society want to find out what is beyond the mind, what is beyond the brain, what is beyond time and space. Their attraction to meditation is for the transcendence of time and space, transcendence of the mind; and mind being matter, transcendence of matter. So this seems to be the nature of the urge that takes you from your country to faraway countries, to Tibetan lamas, to Hindu sannyasis, to Buddhist monks, to so-called yogis, to people who claim to do shaktipatas—transformation of power and shakti—and so on.

This is the nature of the urge, and I think that it is an auspicious symptom of the days to come that man is exploring the dimensions of life beyond time and space, beyond the physical and the cerebral, and so on. We will go into these issues gradually, step by step, but before we proceed to these very serious issues of life, I would like to bring to the notice of every one of you that for transcendence to take place, or to occur, order is absolutely necessary on the level of the physical, the verbal, and the cerebral. If the physical, the verbal, or the cerebral life is disorderly; if there is chaos in the sphere of emotion, sentiment, or feeling; if there is anarchy in the region of thoughts, ideas, or values; if there is disorder in the simple things of daily life, such as diet, such as sleep, such as taking exercise; if there is disorder in a simple matter such as breathing, then if you try to build up a structure of exploration on the basis of this disorder, it is like building a house on the sand. The house should be built on rock, on the solid foundation of inner order, physical, verbal, and cerebral. We live in disorder. Our lives are very disorderly, and we live casually. From morning till night, we move only when an outside compulsion whips us and obliges us to move. If there is a job to do, if there is business to take care of, if there is an engagement, then the whip of compulsion obliges us to live physically, verbally, or cerebrally. Otherwise our lives pass in inertia. We do things whenever we like, as we like, as we dislike, doing things, not doing things: everything is so casual.

So casualness, postponement, lethargy, sluggishness, and laziness: all these overwhelm our daily lives, which is what we have got here on this Earth. If a person feels that his physical life can be disorderly, and that he can use speech in any way he likes, then there is no connection between the motive in the mind and the words that are spoken, no link between the words that are spoken and the actions that are taken. If there are gaps everywhere, if there are pits everywhere, and we go hopping over pits, neglecting them, dodging them, ignoring them, explaining them away, or wishing them away, then this urge to explore that which is beyond time and space will remain only a wish in the mind, a pious wish, a pious intention.

So as a friend who has taken the voyage and is still on the voyage, who launched upon the voyage very early in life, I would like to attract your attention to this issue of putting the house in order first, putting the house of your own life in order so that the physical structure, the body, is as healthy as it is capable of being. I say "as healthy as it is capable of being" because the question of inheritance comes in, the constitutional idiosyncrasies that you inherit, the constitutional built-in weaknesses, the distortions that you inherit. They may be there. So you need to have a body that is healthy, that is subtle, as much as it is possible for your particular body to be healthy and to be in that nimble, pliable, subtle condition: if you have not learned it, then it is better to learn it first. Don't take a vow—this I must eat and this I must not eat, and I must sleep for six hours or I must not sleep—not the musts and must nots, not the oughts and ought nots. This educational matter is to be taken care of by each individual for himself or herself in order to find out and to provide the body with the necessary sleep, with the necessary diet, with the necessary exercises. Why should the body become a problem? Why should there be rigidity in the body? Why should speech be a problem? Do you know what I mean?

Many people say, "Oh, I don't mean this, I mean that." They mean one thing, but they say something else. There is no clarity, no precision, no accuracy in verbal expression. Vagueness pervades the speech. Why? Why not learn to say precisely what you mean? Why not say exactly what you imply? Why play hide and seek with verbal expressions? Why indulge in vague exaggerations, understatements, and overstatements? You know, you distort speech: unhealthy speech, distorted speech, which is what lying and falsehood is. So one has to live the verbal life. To speak, to communicate, is one of the most important actions and movements of life. Make your speech orderly, so that it flows easily and gracefully in accordance, in harmony, with your motive, with your implications, without any distortion, understatement, or overstatement. One whose speech flows smoothly and in harmony with his motives and intentions is a fearless person. So this is the educational part. One has to have a harmonious relationship with speech. This is the foundation of meditation.

The foundation of meditation, the foundation of the noncerebral exploration that one wants to make, is a way of life. So in a nondogmatic way, one has to find out what is agreeable to one's physical structure, learning and growing in rhythm. I hope you appreciate the difference between discipline and the inner order of rhythm. When you do something without understanding its meaning, its significance, and its relationship to your total life, it becomes a discipline, an imposition. Then you have to follow it, whether you impose it upon yourself or somebody else imposes it upon you, or you accept it on the authority of others. When you understand the implications and the relationship of that particular to the whole of your life, then it is no longer a discipline. Then it is a rhythm. It is a rhythm, it is an inner order, which is no burden to your mind, whether conscious, subconscious, or unconscious. Discipline causes a psychological burden when you accept a form of discipline because you are accepting it on authority. Discipline, accepted discipline, becomes more and more of a burden because every day there is a resistance to that discipline, there is a friction in your mind, and there is no harmony. I hope that this point is clear. I was born in India. Suppose I am told that I must get up at 4 o'clock in the morning, somebody tells me, "Getting up at 4 o'clock is very holy, very sacred," and you meditate at that time and so on and so on. I do not ask why getting up at 4 o'clock is so holy and sacred: I accept it. The next day, I have an alarm clock by my side, and at 4 o'clock there is the alarm bell and I say, "Oh, now I have to get up, it is 4 o'clock." There is resistance: I do not want to get up, but I tell myself that I must get up because sitting in silence, or meditating, at 4 o'clock is supposed to be very helpful. This is the sacred time full of nectar; I must get up. So this is the acceptance of authority; I want to follow authority. You want to follow something only when there is a resistance to it somewhere: otherwise there is no following, there is only doing it. So the next morning, there is a resistance and I say, "No, I must do it." So I drag my body out of bed.

Resistance has caused friction. There is a very subtle irritation in the nervous system and also in the chemical system, and I force my body to sit up in so-called silence, or meditation. So you see that in discipline there is a resistance, there is a friction and a lack of harmony. But when you understand why you have to get up at 4 o'clock or 6 o'clock or 7 o'clock, then you sit right up with the spinal cord straight and the neck erect and so on. Why do you do it? If you find out the relationship of that question to the total inquiry, then chances are that there will be no resistance or irritation. That is why I use the term "inner order." Inner order is the result of your spontaneous action out of understanding; discipline is something that you force upon yourself because the intellect accepts an idea. The intellect accepts an idea, the brain forces it upon the physical structure, and so there is resistance and irritation and friction, and you have a sense of being imprisoned in the discipline. You feel as if you are a prisoner of your own mind, of your own brain, of your own intellect.

You are the prison-house, you are the prisoner, and you are the one who imprisons yourself: it goes like that. That is why I say each person has to find out how to put his own house in order, what to eat and what not to eat, when to eat and when not to eat, how much to eat and how to provide the necessary proteins and starches and vitamins to the body, and how many hours to sleep. You may discuss things with one person or ten people, you may read books, but the ultimate result is to be your own. So it is no longer a decision requiring an effort of will, it is no longer a vow taken by you; but, naturally and easily, you grow into a new way of rhythm.

So order is the foundation of an exploration of what is beyond time and space, what is beyond matter. The relationship with matter—that is, your own body and your own brain—has to be orderly. Please do see the importance of this. If the science of yoga has anything at all to teach modern man, it is this necessity of living life in an orderly fashion. And one has to go about it easily and gracefully; without compulsions or violence; without losing one's freedom, without losing one's own initiative, and without losing the balance of the body, or the poise of the mind. One has to educate the mind, the speech, and the body into a new way of living. This education is absolutely necessary.

That which is beyond time and space cannot be explored only through verbal speculation and academic discussion. Meditation is a very serious matter, not a sad matter, but a very serious matter. So anyone who has attachment to traditional patterns of living has to wake up; anyone who has attachment to habit patterns has to wake up and see what that attachment does to his or her life.

There is a second point that one would like to suggest in this introductory talk today, this mere introduction to the attitude toward spiritual inquiry and attitude toward meditation as a new dimension of life. The second point that one would like to share with you today is this: in the new exploration, the old forms of energy and the old patterns of movement may be absolutely irrelevant. You and I have a way of moving and a way of using energy: physical energy, mental energy, verbal energy. Our movement on all the planes—physical, verbal, and mental—implies the use of energy in a certain channel. You know, life is to live and to move in relationship. And to move in relationship, you have to use energy. You use energy. You move physically in space and time. You move through your words, you move through your thoughts. So traditionally we have been educated to move in relationships and use the energy available to us in certain channels.

I hope you remember what we talked about previously: energy is the property of matter. Movement is possible wherever there is energy, and energy is the property of matter. So whether you move through your body within time and space, or you move through your thoughts and ideas and feelings and sentiments, or whether you move through acquiring experiences—sensual, extrasensory, occult, or transcendental; as long as you are moving and using energy, you are in the field of matter, time, and space. All movement is within the sphere of matter, time, and space. The very idea of movement, the very concept of movement and measuring movement, the very concept of time and space, is the creation of the human mind.*

*The closing part of this talk could not be recorded due to failure of electricity.

CHAPTER FIVE

The Silence of Meditation

Mount Abu; July 18, 1973

As we saw the other day, energy is matter in motion. We cannot see, feel, or experience energy unless matter is put into motion. In the same way, thought is mind put into motion. Experiencing is the conditioned mind put into motion. Wherever the thought mechanism is functioning, wherever and whenever experiencing is taking place, it is an indication that the mind is in motion. It is a movement of the mind, in the mind, and measured by the mind, whether individual or collective. This is very important to remember, because these days it is a fashion to look upon meditation as a movement of the mind into the unknown.

Meditation is looked upon as the state of experiencing something that is nonsensual. Thinking or experiencing has the ego, the self, the me, the I, at the center. It is a movement from the center outward: the center moving out toward the frontiers of its own structure. Thinking as a response of memory, or experiencing as a response of the whole conditioning, is a movement of the ego, the self, the me, toward the frontiers of its own structure. Awareness is a movement of the intelligence; it is the sensitivity of the whole human being moving out of the individual toward the cosmos. It is not an ego-centered movement. It is not a movement of the I, the self, the me; it is not the projection of the conditioned psyche; it is not the projection of human experience, either acquired or inherited, contained in the subconscious or the unconscious. As long as there is thinking and experiencing, projection does take place. When there is awareness, it is a movement not from the brain, not from the head, but from the whole individual: the sensitivity, the intelligence, permeates the whole individual, moving out in receptivity toward the cosmos. Awareness requires two things: a person who is in the state of awareness, and that which is independent of the person, of which he is aware. So even in awareness there is motion. There is movement, indicating that there is energy. Those of you who have studied the whole game of the conditioned human psyche—thought, feeling, sentiment, experience, and memory—and those of you who have seen the whole game of the center—the me, the I—referring to the past and projecting the past onto the present, are aware of the meaning of an experience. According to the brilliance of the intellect, according to the quality of the intellect, a person modifies the past, qualifies the past, and projects it onto the present. This is experiencing. You recognize the present in terms of the past, in terms of the known, in terms of the experiences acquired by you or by the collective human race. So it is a movement of the known from the known toward the unknown. The movement of the known from the center, with its whole known inheritance, is the content of the human consciousness. That content provides the momentum for the center to move out toward the unknown. So it is the movement of the known, with the help of the known, toward the unknown. It is the movement of the conditioned human psyche, with the help of all the conditionings, toward that which is unconditioned. That is experience. That is thought. That is how you get ideas. That is how you get imagination. That is how you improvise new thoughts and new values, coin new ideas, and arrive at new conclusions.

But awareness is the unconditioned psyche. It is the unconditioned intelligence contained in the human being. It is not owned by the person. It is not personally acquired by the individual. Awareness is the unconditioned, uncontaminated energy moving out from the individual toward the unknown. And because intelligence has no past and because intelligence is not conditioned, it hasn't got words to verbalize that which it encounters. So intelligence says that life is infinite. It says that there is immortality. It says that there is eternity. It says that God is indescribable and immeasurable. Intelligence, being unconditioned, uninherited, and uncontaminated, has no words. So when you ask a person to talk about liberation, satori, or an encounter with cosmic life, or universal life, he puts it into negative terms because he does not find the words, but still there is an urge to communicate. To verbalize, he has to refer to the substratum of intelligence, the substratum of intelligence being the intellect, the brain, the mind, the conditionings, the inheritance, and so on. When he refers to the substratum of intelligence, in reaction it gives not the synonym but the opposite of the synonym. If he calls this world limited, he calls the other unlimited. If he refers to this life between birth and death as mortal, he refers to the other as immortal. He has no other words. He has to use the antonyms of the words that are contained in the conditioned psyche. The unconditioned intelligence has no language: it only feels. Awareness has no language, being born of duality, the tensions of the me and the not me, the I and the it, the I and the thou. So it has no language, and the words used in every language by the mystics and the so-called self-realized boil down to "It is not this, this is not it." So when the unconditioned nonpersonal intelligence moves as a state of awareness, it seems to refer indirectly to the conditioned psyche. In thought and experience, there is a direct reference and you draw upon it. In awareness, the intelligence refers to it negatively, indirectly. Thus awareness is obviously not the state of meditation.

As long as there is motion, energy is moving in the field of matter. Without matter, there is no motion. Please do see this. Unless there is matter, some kind of matter, gross or subtle, there can be no motion, there can be no movement. When I move from this place to the door, you know what that movement or motion implies. There are two points: here and there. When I move from here, even a step or two, I am not here. The motion requires space, time, and matter. There are two ends in every motion from here to there. Life being an indivisible, homogeneous whole, there are no points in it to move from here to there. It is only in the realm of a consciousness, conditioned as well as unconditioned, that motion is possible. Meditation is a state where the human consciousness, unconditioned and conditioned, spontaneously ceases to operate. Meditation is a state of being where intellect as well as intelligence cease to move outward from their centers. That is why all efforts to acquire new experience through the mind are irrelevant to meditation. All efforts to acquire something new—new thoughts, new ideas, new experiences, new visions, whether sensual or extrasensual, occult, transcendental, or mystical—are irrelevant to the state of meditation. And awareness that "I," as an individual, "am" in harmony with the total, with the universal, with the cosmos, is also irrelevant. The awareness between the "I" and the "it" is also a very subtle movement, a very subtle motion that conditions it. I wonder if I can make this point and communicate it properly: awareness of oneself as independent of the universe, being in harmony or disharmony with the universe, is also an experience that conditions. Mystical experiences condition you as much as sensual experiences do. Thoughts, good or bad, condition us; and experiences, good or bad, sensual, sexual, nonsensual, or occult, all condition the mind. This sustains duality, and meditation is a state in which there is no duality, not even an awareness of nonduality. When I say that I am aware of the nonduality of life, I am still trying to sustain the individual, the entity, as separate from and independent of the rest of life. The awareness of nonduality also conditions you. Somebody says "I am the body" and somebody else says "I am Brahman" but the "I" is there. So I wonder if you can see with me that even the movement of unconditioned, nonpersonal intelligence as awareness is not meditation.

The world is moving very fast today from the biological and the material, the economic and the political, toward the psychological, the cerebral, the occult, and the mystical. There is a definite movement of the global human mind toward the invisible, toward the occult, toward the mystical and transcendental. There is no doubt about it. And that is why one has to be extremely cautious. Meditation is becoming a global fashion, the latest mode of the human psyche, like a hairdo and clothes. The word *meditation* is becoming psychic slang, and I say this with great pain, because it is something that cannot be dragged down to the level to which it is being dragged. So anyone who promises you new experiences or new visions in the name of meditation is tempting you to move away from the integrity of your inquiry.

There are techniques and methods that pacify the mind and soothe the nerves, techniques to teach you relaxation, and they have their own utility. I have nothing against them. If somebody helps you to concentrate by focusing your attention upon a subject and sustaining it there, that is a part of education. It will sharpen your mind. It will enrich your memory. It has its own utility, but if somebody offers it in the name of meditation, then one is being misled. If somebody promises astral traveling, lights and visions, manifest and unmanifest sounds, and the rest of it, these are romantic adventures in the invisible world. But the occult or the transcendental does not become real only because it is invisible, only because it is intangible. One who is inquiring what life is, one who is inquiring what silence is, what meditation is, or what freedom is, has to see that in meditation there is no concentration, observation, or attention; there is not even awareness.

It is only when the awareness of the self as the I being in harmony with the universe subsides of its own that silence comes to life. Till then, there may be quietness, there may be peacefulness, but there is no silence. So the spontaneous cessation of movement on the part of the conditioned human psyche as well as the unconditioned human psyche is the content of silence. The individual then is no longer an entity that is separate from the rest of life, any more than a cloud that floats in the sky is. The cloud has a shape. It has a form, but not a center, nor an identity. So, too, the human being in the dimension of silence may have a form, a shape, a body consisting of flesh and bones and nerves and blood; and yet there is no entity in the sense that there is no center. Such an individual has no center left in the conditioned or the unconditioned psyche. There is no center. The individual then is like a bubble on the waters of a river or a lake or an ocean. The bubble contains water, is born in water, is made of water, and subsides into water. So the form of such an individual contains that nondualistic silence, that centerless silence, and when the form subsides, you call it death. The silence, the nonduality, becomes again an organic part of the universal: silence and nonduality.

And one would like to proceed with this subject and say that such a state of silence is possible. It can be contained in this human form and the human being can live in that dimension without any break, without any interruption. A drum contains silence and inside the drum there is only space, but when somebody touches the drum, it gives out a tone. In the same way, relationships touch the individual and the response comes out of the silence. The response comes from neither the conditioned nor the unconditioned: the response is born of silence. The response born in that silence has to travel through the intelligence and use the intellect in order to get expressed. That is a different matter. Just as the space contained in the drum has to travel through the leather in order to give you a tone, a note, in the same way that state of silence percolating through the intelligence, using the intellect, the brain, the mind, expresses itself in relationship. But while being percolated through the intelligence and the intellect, it retains the quality of that nondualistic silence, it retains the freshness of the nonpersonal, frontierless life. I wish that I could tell you how the state of silence moving into relationship or responding to relationship, is then the content of life. Notice that I am using the term "silence," I am not yet calling it "meditation." I am calling it the state of silence that responds to relationships, responds to challenges, with nonpersonal freshness. Do you know what nonpersonal freshness is? An individual's body can be fresh: all the muscles, the glands, the nerves can be very healthy. There is freshness. A person's mind can be fresh: up to date, well informed, well cultivated, and acquainted with all the current fashionable thoughts and ideologies and cerebral ways of behavior. Then there can be the freshness of an intelligence that is always communing with the universal, with the cosmic; this also is freshness. Personal freshness, that is to say, freshness limited by the person, and nonpersonal freshness have different qualities altogether. A person living in the state of silence gives out a sense of nonpersonal freshness in every relationship. We shall proceed from this point in a later session.

Suffice it to say today that meditation is not a pursuit of the intellect or the intelligence. It is not a movement from the center toward the frontiers or beyond the frontiers.

Before we depart this afternoon, I will leave with you one more point: the distinction between movement and vibration. When you say that there is a movement, horizontal movement or vertical movement, it is between two points. But when there are vibrations, the vibrations have no direction, no polarity of two points. The vibration is not from here to there. It is like inhaling and exhaling the breath: it is a motiveless, directionless happening. The distinction between movement and vibration must be understood clearly. Can we imagine horizontal and vertical movement together? When you move, you move either horizontally or vertically; in a vibration, however, the vertical and horizontal get together. In vibration, there is simultaneity of the horizontal and vertical. Life vibrates. It does not move. Meditation seems to me to be the state of the is-ness of life, the to-be-ness of life.

CHAPTER SIX

In the Spirit of Inquiry

Mount Abu; July 19, 1973

This is going to be a discussion meeting. I request that the friends who have come from abroad communicate their questions, ask for clarification of what has been said if they need any, and give their comments, if any. A discussion is a participative inquiry. Individuals who are seriously and sincerely interested in finding out the meaning of life come together and communicate with one another. A question or a problem, if it is not borrowed from books, if it is not imposed upon you, due to the ambition to acquire some new experience, if it is born of the soil of your relationships, if it is a flower that blossoms in your own heart, has always a universal content.

It is not easy to have a genuine problem. You have *to live* in order to have a challenge or a problem. If you hesitate, then there are no questions. If you accept the authority either of the ancient or the modern scriptures and interpretations of ancient or modern so-called prophets, teachers, or masters, then there will be no questions. When there is a challenge or a problem to be faced, it indicates that the person is living alertly and attentively. An absentminded student in a class has no questions, no doubts. And a student who is concerned only with passing the examinations and attends the class in order to fulfill the demands of the school, for his presence at roll call, has no doubts. He is concerned with being present because his presence is demanded. He sits in class and hears, instead of listening to the words of the teacher. You must *live* in order to have a challenge. So one who asks a question, who poses a problem, who makes an inquiry born of sacred and holy doubt, thus enriches the minds of other participants. This is psychic intercourse among human beings of different races, brought up in different cultures, and living in different condition-ings; it is a very enriching experience.

A discussion can take place when there is no dogmatism in the minds either of the speaker or of the listeners, when the approach is one of nim-ble and tender tentativeness. If there were a claim on the part of any one of us that he knew the whole truth or he understood the whole truth, then there could not be any discussion. Then there would be only a pre-tense of a discussion. There would be a question-and-answer meeting as if the person who sat on the platform had all the answers to all the prob-lems of the whole human race. This pretense would be audacious. So let us feel very free, as there will be more discussion meetings and this is only the beginning. Let us understand that the purpose of a discussion is not to show off one's knowledge or to make assertions about one's experiences or to make efforts to convince and convert others: but rather, it is a friendly gesture.

You raise a question and I take it for granted that you have looked at the question from more angles than one, and I try to look at it in the light of my own understanding. Petal by petal, the question, the problem, begins to unfold itself, and all of us look at it. To understand the implications of the question and to relate them to the whole of your life is to nearly arrive at the answer to the question. The solution to a problem does not lie out-side the problem nor does it lie somewhere else, that is to say, outside the individual. The solution is neither outside the problem nor is it outside the individual. After all, every individual is a condensed universe. Every indi-vidual is the whole universe condensed into this human form. So please don't feel that you are here to ask questions of me, hoping that I know the answers and that I am going to dish them out to you. We shall look at the questions, look at the problems. There will be no hurry on our part to arrive at the answer, but every care will be taken to look at the question fearlessly, to look at it for the joy of looking at it, for the joy of under-standing it: it is great fun, you know. It is great fun when friends sit to-gether and feel free to discuss. With this background in mind, let us now proceed with the discussion. If there is any difficulty with the language, don't feel shy. You can go slowly, find the words, and express yourself.

[At this point, Vimala responds to a participant's question.]

This friend says that you need a power of inquiry in order to discover the truth. Now, in the United States many of us are turning away from affluence and materialism toward a spiritual inquiry. He says, Is this not a reaction?

It *can* be a reaction, and with many, it *is* a reaction. The cultural problems of affluence, the inner contradictions contained in affluence, began to manifest themselves after World War II. The economic imperialism of the United States began spreading after World War II and it became a very powerful country, militarily, politically, and economically. If it is a reaction to all this, it will lead the individual toward personal escape and refuge. It will take the young inquirer to various countries in the East and the West to find out a new sensational field to work upon. And the occult and the transcendental is a very romantic, uncharted ocean.

The romance with the occult is mistaken for a spiritual inquiry. Thus the reaction can lead a person to travel to far-off Eastern countries, and take to austerities and rituals that are not part of his or her own culture. If it is a reaction, then inquiry comes to an end within a short time and the person finds gratification in some form of escape. Whether it is a reaction to affluence or to starvation, as it is in India, reactions haven't got much momentum. They can't sustain the depth and intensity of inquiry.

Now the second part of the question seems to be, Is inquiry born naturally? Does it not happen sometimes that a person goes through an event that makes him full of sorrow, an event that shakes him to his very roots? It may be an astounding success—unexpected success or affluence arrived at suddenly and abruptly—that shakes the person. It may be failure or frustration that shakes a person completely, turns everything constructed by his mind topsy-turvy. Sometimes a beloved person departs from the world and your whole evaluation of life goes through a radical change. Doesn't an inquiry get stimulated by events that descend upon you suddenly, abruptly, unexpectedly, and you feel incapable of meeting them squarely and totally? An inquiry may be caused by such abrupt, sudden happenings in life. The inquirer hidden in each human heart comes to the forefront when a person comes face-to-face with sorrow. The psychological suffering that he cooks up out of the event, the self-pity, the depression, do not satisfy him: somewhere, something is missing. So even after having gone through the stimulated self-suffering, he arrives at sorrow face-to-face and maybe sorrow stimulates inquiry. Many a time love can stimulate an inquiry.

Thirdly, as you have mentioned, some individuals are born with an urge toward inquiry. I do not know about other individuals, but you have referred to my life. It seems to me that the inquiry that first expressed itself when I was five years old was one that I inherited. My grandfather was an inquirer himself. He had studied yoga and led the life that was nearly that of a yogi. So it could be a biological and a psychological inheritance. When individuals seem to be born with it, it is not that they are extraordinary or the chosen few of the divine. Maybe there is this issue of inheritance, a psychological and psychic inheritance that goes back many generations.

Now we come to the last part of the question: If an individual is not born with it, and if an individual does not find the inquiry stimulated by the failures or the successes of his life, by the sorrows or the joys of his life, it is possible for him to arrive at this inquiry?

It is not only possible for every individual, but inquiry is hidden in almost every human heart. We human beings try to dodge the inquiry, suppress the inquiry, push it into the background, and say to ourselves, *Well, I will find out the truth in old age: this is not the time to do it.* The inquiry whispers to us right from childhood. I wonder if, in the company of children, you have ever alertly and attentively listened to their questions: whether the children are born in India or the United States or Australia does not make any difference. If their inquiries are not suppressed, children have questions about God, sex, death, and life; about the sun, the moon, and the stars. Grown-ups have no time to look at the questions of children; those questions are looked upon as academic questions, even though children do not have any academic questions. They are the vibrations of the pure, innocent mind trying to open up and receive the meaning of life.

We have artificially created a society in which we have become victims of the speed that we ourselves have created. We have created it in the name of culture, civilization, and the development of science and technology. We have created cities that are monstrously huge. We have created units of production, also monstrously huge, where human beings become dehumanized and depersonalized. We have an economic structure where the consumer never meets the producer. So production has lost its charm and consumption has lost its grace. The workers meet in the factory not as individuals, as persons, but as the boss, the peon, the engineer, the merchant, the salesman, the agent, and so on. Thus the whole structure is such that we have no time to live as whole human beings, meeting one another as total human beings. The teacher meets the student, instead of the grown-up meeting the grown-up. This is why we have no time to listen to the questions of children, no time to play with them, or even to look at them. This is why the inquiry, which is bubbling and struggling to get verbalized in the minds of children, gets suppressed; instead, the child is taught to ask questions that have a utility, that have a practical value. The dichotomy between practical life and life as a whole is imposed upon a child by the age of four or five. So please don't think that this inquiry is unique to some exceptional individuals. Some may have the aspect of inheritance in their favor that others may not have. But inquiry is there in each human heart. When we grow up and the questions begin to whisper, we say, *This is not the time: I have to pass my examinations; I have to find a job; I must have the standard of living that my neighbor has, that my cousin has.* Thus we go on pushing the inquiry into the background. The inquiry into the meaning of life—what death is, what living is—is natural. The inquiry is the call of the divine vibrating in the human heart.

There is one more thing that I would like to share with you. We have been taught and trained—I cannot use the word *educated*, because we are not educated—physically and mentally, to love money, to respect money, prestige, and power, as well as to love and worship security. There is no atmosphere where children can grow with the love of life. Anyone who loves living is given ready-made formulas in the name of ethics, religion, metaphysics, economics, political philosophy, codes of conduct, and sets of values. So we do not grow in an atmosphere where living is looked upon as something holy, sacred, where every movement of life is something to be understood. If there is anger coming up in my mind or jealousy getting whipped up by my ego or violence boiling in my heart, I do not know how to look at the anger or the jealousy, because I have all the ready-made solutions. The encounter with the anger or with the violence boiling up within me does not take place. The moment it is coming up, we refer to the books, the tradition, the authority, or the scriptures.

We are afraid of life. This fear of life and fear of death does not allow the inquiry to get articulated. The inquiry is not unique. It is there, provided one has the courage to look at it and not push it into the background, no matter the cost. And if a person responds to the inquiry and turns his face toward truth, life, and reality, then his relatives, friends, and neighbors feel that something is wrong with him. They fail to understand why instead of earning money and instead of indulging in one pleasure after another in sequence, the person turns his face toward truth. The person is looked upon as some peculiar crazy animal not conforming to the order of priorities of society. So in order not to be laughed at by society, one keeps such inquiries and doubts nicely in a box, to be opened in old age. Many times, the box accompanies the person to the grave. It is never opened.

[At this point, Vimala responds to another participant's remarks.]

There was a phrase used by my friend here, "the smokeless flame of inquiry." He also used the words "the purity of inquiry without a motive." When there is an inquiry, the utilitarian mind says, *Well, what is the practical value of understanding the meaning of life? Can the meaning of life be cashed? Supposing that I understand what reality is, supposing that I arrive at meditation, which is the state of unconditional silence, what then? What does society get out of it and what do I get out of it?* When the consideration that one has to get something out of the answer is there, then the inquiry is not pure.

Whenever there is a motive to get something, acquire something, obtain something extraordinary and exceptional, the inquiry gets contaminated: the eyes get clouded and the ears get blocked. We fall into the net of those who are out to fish for their organizations. It is our motive that creates the net for those who are out to exploit others. Through the hands of someone else, we are victimized by our own motives. Someone who does not want anything from anyone can never be exploited, however alluring the propaganda may be. No promises, no blueprints, and no schemes can crush him. The purity of inquiry implies the willingness to learn. Learning is growing; learning is living. A motiveless inquiry has no utility. Therefore it cannot be exploited. It is the arrogance of the self, the me, the I, the ego, going out to acquire something in the name of liberation, satori, or meditation, that gets exploited.

So one has to ask oneself, *Why am I doing this? If I want new powers of the mind, then let me be honest and confess that I want powers of the mind; I am troubled by mental problems and I want someone to give me methods and techniques to soothe the mind.* There are many psychological therapists and psychic therapists. But therapy has nothing to do with meditation. If I want that, let me have it honestly and frankly, as a psychological therapy or as a psychic therapy. Just as with troubled bodies and physical structures, so, too, there are ways of pacifying, soothing, and relaxing troubled minds. But the technique for relaxation is not meditation. Thus it is humility that keeps the inquiry innocent and pure. Maybe when you discover the truth, the body, the mind, and the brain get transformed and you have a different grace, a different freshness, and a different energy. Maybe this happens. But this is a by-product; this is a side effect.

In the state of meditation, is one aware of one's body and the surroundings? Is one aware that one is in the state of meditation?

While you are listening to me or speaking to me, are you aware of the breathing process that is taking place in your body? You are listening now; you are also inhaling and exhaling breath: are you aware of it? Secondly, does that inhaling and exhaling require an effort of the me? Please do understand the question. Does the inhaling and the exhaling take place from the center of the I, the me? Is it an activity of the me, the self, the ego? Are you aware of it? All of us breathe. Are you aware of the breathing that is taking place? It is a complex process: inhaling, retaining, and exhaling. It is taking place all the time, while you are awake and while you are sleeping. Does it require an effort, a conscious effort, to inhale or exhale?

Marie is listening to me. Mark and Joral are listening to me. Is Joral, during the one hour that she is listening to me, aware that she is Joral? Is Mark aware that he is Mark? Is Bob aware that he is Bob? What happens to your name and your form while you are listening? We will inquire into the state of meditation later on; but right now, let us deal with the field of the known. When you learn pranayama, you are very conscious of the deep breathing. When you breathe deeply and retain it, you become conscious that you have retained the breath and you exhale it slowly. You are very conscious of it. You are listening to the music, the sitar. While you are listening to the music here, are you aware of your body and of your surroundings? How is your awareness of your body and surroundings related to your awareness of the music? Is your awareness of your body and surroundings an organic part of your awareness of the music? Or are these two different awarenesses? I am aware of the body, and I am aware of the music. Do they exist side by side, or do they form a homogeneous whole?

Do you understand my question? We are trying to look at the question posed earlier from a different angle altogether. When you understand the known, then the other is easy to understand. So before going into the issue of what happens in meditation, let us find this out: otherwise, our discussion of meditation will be mere speculation.

CHAPTER SEVEN

The Realm of Nonduality

Mount Abu; July 20, 1973

Do you remember the question that we discussed yesterday? Does any one of you remember the question at all? Somebody asked a question and I asked you certain questions in return. Do you remember them? Let us recollect the whole thing precisely.

Look, somebody said to me, in the state of meditation, is there an "I" consciousness, is there awareness of the body and of the surroundings, and is there awareness that one is in the state of meditation? Will you please tell me what happens to your "I" consciousness and your awareness of your body and of your surroundings while you are listening to me? While you are listening, what happens to your breathing? Is it an activity of the ego, the self, the me? Are you conscious that you are breathing? Are you conscious of your name, of your body, and so on? Let us discuss what happens to us when we are listening here and now, instead of trying to imagine what happens in the state of meditation.

Let us find out what happens here. Now what do you say? This friend says that it depends upon the degree of your attention and the degree of being absorbed by what is being said. If one is completely absorbed in what one is listening to, then there is no awareness of the body or the breathing process or the surroundings. Is this not what you are saying? And if one is not much interested in or not attending to what is being said totally, then one becomes aware of the surroundings. One has a choice either to focus attention upon what is being said or to think about oneself and the surroundings. We have to take it for granted for the sake of verbal communication that you are listening attentively and unconditionally; that you are interested in what is being said.

You must have listened to the talks of many persons, and you must have listened to music. What happens to you? Have you ever watched? In intense listening, this friend says, there is an awareness, but the "I" consciousness does not function. There is an awareness of the surroundings. There is an awareness that something is being spoken. There is an awareness that one is in the state of listening. And that is all. We have to look at it. It does not matter if we falter, if we commit mistakes, or if the observation is inaccurate. The moment that we make an inaccurate observation and we understand that it is inaccurate, that very inaccuracy leads to accuracy. But if we are afraid and inhibited by fear that we will be inaccurate, then we will be imprecise; the fear of imprecision and inaccuracy will not let us work at all, will not let us operate at all. The fear of inaccuracy and imprecision—the fear of committing mistakes—will paralyze the psychic action. So please don't feel afraid.

If we are to find out what happens to us when we are in the act of listening, in the midst of deep listening, then we must ask, *Am I aware of the breathing process? Am I aware of the body, of my name, that I am a man, that I am a woman, that I come from Canada or the United States, or the Netherlands, or Bombay, that I am wearing certain types of clothes? Am I aware that I am listening?* Are you aware of the speaker: his or her form, clothes, features, voice, words? What are you aware of? What I am trying to attract your attention to is that consciousness going completely into abeyance does not paralyze the movement of life. The "I" consciousness goes into abeyance: you may not be aware of your body, of your name, of your form, or of your clothes. You are in the midst of the communication, something being communicated to you, and through the words you find the meaning and the communication is of the meaning of God; words are only the vehicles to communicate something or symbols to indicate something.

When you pronounce the word *cow,* there is actually a cow, an animal, in existence, and the word *cow* is only a symbol to indicate the existence of the cow actually in life. So when you utter the word *cow,* the word has a meaning, and the listener understands the meaning. So the word *cow* is only a vehicle, a conveyance, for the transportation of the meaning of life: the transportation of meaning takes place through words. Words are vehicles that convey something, provided that you are listening, not hearing: hearing is an involuntary activity of the ears, the auditory nerves; it is beyond your control. As long as you are alive, your ears are bound to hear.

Hearing is different from listening. In hearing, the attention is diffused. But in listening, it gets focused on one point. So when you are listening, you don't listen as Devayani or Joral or Marie, and yet the body is there, the name is there, and the "I" consciousness is there; they have not been destroyed. They are fully capable of functioning whenever the necessity arises.

So now we proceed to the point of meditation. The body, the physical structure, has a built-in way of surviving or functioning, as I hope you have noticed. When you listen to music or to a speech, when you watch a game of football or cricket being played by experts, when you watch tenderly with love or with great concern, the action of audition or perception is taking place. The built-in process of the physical structure goes on working by itself: the hearing, the seeing, the breathing, and the registering of various names and forms does go on. You don't have to make an effort to hold your body straight when you sit down to listen to a talk. You don't have to make an effort to breathe in or breathe out. There is a guarantee in the subconscious mind that you can inhale and exhale. So the inhaling and exhaling go on without your conscious effort. There is a conscious effort if you are suffering from asthma. If you have lung trouble and you sit down to listen to a talk or to write something or to read something, then you have to make a conscious effort to breathe. When there is an abnormality, when there is a disability, when there is a sickness, then you immediately become aware of the breathing process. You become aware that you are sitting when you have pain in some parts of the body. Suppose that you have a pain in the knee or in the neck or in the ankle, and you are listening to a talk. In between the awareness, the pain reminds you of your body: that you have a body and the body is finding it difficult to sit down or to breathe. But otherwise, without the "I" consciousness making an effort, the body goes on functioning.

There is a built-in process, a process incorporated into the biological structure, that does not need an effort of the will at all. In the same way, there is a built-in process in the psychological structure: now, as you are sitting here in the hall, your body is in contact with the ground, with the floor, with the carpets that you are sitting upon. There is a foundation and you feel the contact, you feel the solidity of the earth and the floor, and you feel comfortable sitting there.

In the same way, the psychological structure, with the "I," the self, the me, at the center, has the ground of name and forms, colors, and sounds as the floor. The "I" consciousness is aware without a conscious effort. It is aware of your own name, it is aware of your own body and shape, it is aware of the surroundings; the awareness is not an activity of the ego, but as you are now sitting here breathing the air, you are aware of the space and the breeze. You are not attending to the breeze, or to the space in the room, but there is an awareness of the people, of the breeze in the room, and an awareness of the presence of sunshine or clouds or raindrops. The psychological structure has a built-in process; the cerebral organ also has a built-in process.

So in the state of meditation when you are not functioning through the brain, not functioning through the physical structure, the body is still sustained and is capable of unfolding the processes that are built into itself. The "I" consciousness is capable of existing without functioning, existing without operating. It is not damaged, it is not mutilated, but quiet and peaceful; it goes into awareness. In the dimension of silence, there is an awareness of the body as an entity separate from the rest of life, existing independently apart from the universe, apart from its surroundings. Till the dimension of silence, awareness is there.

In the state of meditation, the awareness of the body and of the mind does not persist, does not exist at all. The body functions, just as while you are listening to me, the body functions; without any interference, your body is sitting upright now or in a relaxed way or with stretched legs— whatever you like. It hears, it sees, it breathes. All this is taking place without your making an effort to do the thing. So in the state of meditation, the body moves: it can sit down, it can walk, it can take meals. It can communicate through words when there is a necessity without the "I" consciousness making an effort to eat, to drink, to see, or to walk. Normally when I take meals, I say "I like this thing; I do not like that." I take certain things out of choice. I have likes and dislikes, preferences and prejudices. I have certain norms and criteria inherited from tradition. All these things go into the process of cooking a meal and having it. That is one way. I like it and therefore I eat it, and even when the body says *I have had enough,* because I like the taste, the flavor, the look, the texture, or the consistency of the thing, I eat. All this can happen when I am eating. That is to say, the cooking of the meal and the eating of the meal has a center and has a circumference, a periphery.

Another person living in the state of meditation has to cook a meal, take a meal, wear clothes, wash clothes, talk to people, and meet people, but these activities have not got at the center the I, the me, the self. The I— the Hindu, the Indian, the Swede, or the American—having had this tradition of these likes and dislikes, the whole paraphernalia of the I, does not exist there at the center. The cooking of the meal then has a different meaning altogether. The body has to be fed; it has to be fed in order to keep it healthy. It needs balanced nutrition with good flavor, it needs the meal to be cooked aesthetically. The point of view of nutrition; the approach to beauty, to aesthetics; the consideration of the time that is available; the consideration of the circumstances in which you live; the context of life that you have in society, a poor country such as India or a rich country such as the United States, where you are: the whole awareness is there. So the person cooks a meal and takes it in order to help the body to live elegantly, healthily, and to remain subtle, fresh, and properly fed. So the center is not the I: instead, the center is the relationship of cooking a meal and eating it with your total life and the life around you.

It has the facts of life at the center, not the I. When the person takes a meal and sits at the table, as a cultured person and as an aesthetically keen person—because in meditation the sensitivity is intensified—the efficiency, the competence, the sensitivity, the speed of functioning, the all-inclusiveness of attention to these things, are there, vibrating. So the person sitting at the table will see the meal and have it as a friendship, a harmony, with the physical structure, without being attached to the body or obsessed with the body, neither with the idea of worshiping it, indulging it, nor with the idea of suppressing it, negating it, through austerity or asceticism: "I must eat and I must not eat." Neither the suppression nor the indulgence, neither the worshiping of the body nor the denying of it, the negating of it, calling it a sin: in this way, taking a meal gets related to the whole life.

The relationship of taking a meal to sleep, the relationship of taking a meal to the exercises that you do, to the intellectual work that you do, and to the manual work that you do: the meal gets related to all that. Do you see the frontiers now? The frontiers of cooking a meal or taking a meal go on widening. So one sees the necessities of the body.

Sometimes the body is hungry for starch, sometimes it requires proteins, sometimes it asks for salt and minerals, and sometimes it asks for honey and fruit sugar. Do you listen to the body? So the meal gets directly related to the needs of the body for its health, for its buoyancy, for its freshness, for its vigor, for its vitality. Immediately, the person sees the relationship and takes that, consumes that, in simplicity. In the elements of simplicity, the meals are taken. The relationship with the food—with the liquids or the solids—becomes very simple and direct. The mind does not interfere with, does not get between, the requirements of the physical structure and the food. You know what the mind does when it interferes? *I want to do that. I like this, I don't like that. I have taken this. This was not done in my time. That is not the tradition of my country.* So the mind interferes, obstructs. The simple relationship with life gets complicated when the mind is allowed to interfere.

So in the dimension of meditation, the whole act of living from morning till night and moving through the challenges and relationships of life harmoniously, occurs freely, without any inhibition or any fear. The body and the mind function through built-in intelligence, and there is no conscious effort on the part of the I, the self, the me, to do those activities. The activities do not have, from morning till night, the I at the center.

In the state of meditation, am I aware that I am in the state of meditation? That was the second part. Does that question still remain? Am I aware that I am in the state of meditation? I could be aware that I was in the state of meditation if the activity were born of the I. If it originated from the I, the self, the me, perhaps the complex human consciousness would be aware of that. But it is not born of the I, the me. Have you ever watched a ballet or an ice ballet? If you have ever watched a ballet, a dance performance, if you love watching, then what happens? Your whole body—the nerves, the muscles, the glands—go with the artist. You are not dancing, you are watching the dance. But from a different angle you are with the dance, you are moving with the dance. You are in the midst of the ballet, watching the ballet, and somebody touches your shoulder and you say, "Oh." While you were watching, the movement of the dancer, your "I" consciousness and the movement taking place within your body were all one. They were of one element. There was no dancer and no watcher: it is one movement going backward and forward between the dancer and the person who is watching the dance. You were not aware that you were watching until somebody pats your shoulder and says, "That was beautiful, wasn't it?" Then you are startled. You look back and you feel, or rather, you know, that somebody has done a thing that ought not to have been done. Why did she say that, why did she break the homogeneity of the whole event? Then you become aware that the dancer is there and you are sitting here, that she was dancing and you as a separate person were watching. But till then it was one movement: the dancer, the dance, the person who was watching, and the invisible movement taking place in the body.

Have you ever taken small children to watch a cricket match or other sporting event, or even a speech? A few years ago, I had friends come with me to a seminar in U.P. [Uttar Pradesh]. Their child was a boy about five years old, and this child started imitating the movements of the speaker, who was very fiery. The child was sitting with me, and he would look at the person and, you know, make the same gesture as the speaker. If the speaker would raise his hands, he would raise his hands, too. Now, children can't resist visible movements. They make visible movements. Grown-ups don't make visible movements. But inside them, the movements take place, if they love sports, if they love music, if they love dance.

So the whole—the musician and the listener, the dancer and the spectator, the sound waves of the music and the listener—becomes one movement of life without duality. There is a kind of indivisible homogeneity about the thing. Even when you are listening to a speaker, the speaker, what is being said, the meaning that is being transferred, the listener, and the act of listening become one whole movement, and yet the speaker and the listener are two different persons: they are sitting in two different places with two different bodies; entities do not get destroyed. The homogeneity of the psychic event does not take away the richness of the duality. It is there. On the physical plane and the psychological plane, the duality is there. But the event that takes place occurs in a nonduality, and therefore there is a homogeneity about the whole thing.

This happens for an hour or for a half-hour while you listen to a speech or to music or when you go out for a walk by the seashore or by a lake or on a hilltop; but in the state of meditation, it happens in every moment. The person harmoniously relating to nature by enjoying the trees, the lake, the hills, and the bushes does not become one with the trees and the hills and the bushes. The bushes are there and the hilltops are there. He does not become that. He does not identify himself with that consciousness. And yet there is no duality: the tension of duality does not exist there. Because the perception, the act of perception—the person looking at the lake, the trees, the hilltop—leads the individual from the realm of duality to the realm of nonduality. The joy of this transports you on all levels of your being to the realm of nonduality; not pleasure, but joy. This can happen to you for an hour, for a half-hour, for ten minutes, or for a fraction of a minute, but in the dimension of meditation, it is always there: nonduality, the joy of communion, without destroying the richness of duality. The person eats and drinks and does everything that is required of him, but not from the center of the I.

When you sit down in silence, sit on a piece of cloth, cotton or wool or silk, whatever you have, and use the same piece each time. Then the consistency and intensity of the vibration that is released, that emanates from your body and enters the piece of cloth upon which you sit, that consistency is maintained. It is not disturbed. You know, when you live in a house, you are emanating your thoughts or feelings or sentiments. You emanate a kind of matter from your body. When you look at a person, you are emanating matter, very subtle matter. The act of perception is the act of emanation: something travels from the I to the object of perception. It is very subtle matter. When you receive through the ears, or the auditory nerves, certain sound waves, you are receiving a kind of very subtle matter. Sound waves, or vibrations containing energy, bring into your ears a very subtle kind of matter. When you think a thought, when you feel an emotion, you are emanating things, they affect the walls around you. They affect the things that you use. So use the same piece of cloth each time. This is a scientific approach. One who has studied the science of waves and the relationship of the waves of sound and light and thought and feelings to one's physical structure is very careful about teaching another person about touching things, about using things, and about colors, shapes, and sizes. Everything has an existential eloquence.

Things have their own language. Stone, bricks, lime, cement, earth, and mud: each has its own language to communicate. And while you are in relationship with them, you receive certain things and you give out certain things. The give and take goes on. Why did you say that it was not an important question? You know, life cannot be divided into important and unimportant. There is nothing in life that is small or great; there is nothing less important or more important. Coming to a far-off country, you would like to understand the particulars. Why does she do this? Why does she do that? So it is a very healthy and natural inquiry. Wanting to learn, wanting to find out, just for the fun of it: you are entitled to ask, why should you say that it is not important? I would not sit upon a deerskin if I had to buy it, or if somebody bought it for me, because I would not know whether the animal was shot down or whether it was a natural death and the skin was removed after the animal's death. I did not think of the tradition of using a deerskin, but the tradition may have a point: not everything becomes useless because it goes on out of tradition. Just as not everything can be accepted only because it is traditional, not everything needs to be thrown away outright or condemned if it goes on out of tradition.

The yogis, those who used to learn yoga or to dwell in solitude, lived in a very austere way, a very simple way, living in a cave. Deerskin gave them warmth, electricity and warmth both. So if one has such a piece one can sleep on it and one can sit upon it. That was the only thing that yogis used to have, and they rolled it up and carried it on their shoulders whenever they moved from one place to another. It is like a sleeping bag that you people carry wherever you want. The yogi would not make a distinction between sitting upon the skin while having his meals and sleeping upon it. And I have known of certain yogis having only one piece with them at the height of 10,000 feet in the Himalayas. I went to Gangotri and I was climbing up to the source of the Ganges. After you reach the height of 10,000 feet, you can't carry anything with you. A certain yogi had two such pieces and he would put a string around them and wear them, not just put them around his shoulders. That was protection for his body, and after arriving he would spread one on the ice or the snow and sit upon it, and one would be wrapped around his shoulders. So I have a piece, a very practical thing for an ascetic to have.

Everybody is conditioned. You know, the human race is conditioned, we are conditioned. The content of the human psyche—the knowledge, the experience, the languages, the culture, the civilization, the traditions, everything that is contained in the conscious, the subconscious, and the unconscious—is conditioned.

After all, the content of consciousness is conditioning. That is what we mean by conditioning. The word *conditioning* became very popular in Europe after Pavlov, the Russian psychologist, the founder of the school of behaviorism, used this word. How does man get conditioned? What is human conditioning, and what is animal conditioning? Adherents of the school of behaviorist psychology in Europe included Alfred Adler and Carl Jung, who worked on the theory of behaviorism. Today, *conditioning* is a very fashionable word in the realm of psychology, and has been taken over by metaphysicians, and popularized by J. Krishnamurti. He used and extended the meaning of the word *conditioning* in such a powerful, scientific, and dynamic way that it became a turning point in Western psychology.

Now you are asking, *How can I become aware of conditioning? What happens in conditioning? Do the contents disappear or do they remain there and do they not do any harm to me?* What happens: that is the question. The content of the psyche is the conditioning; the conditionings are the content of our consciousness. Conditioning through education, conditioning through religious background, conditioning through cultural background, conditioning through the social and economic context, conditioning through inheritance, either psychological or biological: conditionings are the content of human consciousness. You cannot throw away your consciousness. Can you? You cannot throw away your skin. You cannot throw away the color of your hair or the color of your skin. You cannot wash it out. You may keep it clean, but you can't wash it out. For example, you have the name Marie given to you by your parents, and now you learn that names are given to identify children and to differentiate one child from another child. I have two children. I give them two different names, Robert and Marie, because I want to distinguish the one from the other. So a name is given, and it has a utility in social relationships. When you understand that, then there is no attachment to the name Marie. When you call Marie, Vimala does not reply; when you call Vimala, Marie does not reply. You are aware that the name Marie is given to this person and the name Vimala is given to that person. Your attachment to the name and your pride and vanity, a kind of glory—all that disappears. The name does not disappear.

When you understand the conditionings as conditionings, then your relationship to conditionings goes through a radical transformation. You are not attached to them, you don't feel glorified by them, and you don't impose these conditionings even upon your own children. You don't measure other human beings by these conditionings. Don't you see how the relationship gets simpler and simpler? It is a very simple relationship. They are there. When you and I meet, what happens to your Christianity and my Hinduism? Where are they? When we meet, we don't meet as Christian and Hindu: we meet as concerned human beings. The Christianity may be there, and the Hinduism may be there. And in certain ways of behavior, certain gestures, the conditionings do express themselves. My hands go up like this when I meet people because this is conditioning, and your hands will go like this to greet your friends. But once you see that this is one form of greeting and this is another form of greeting, then the comparison of the two and the temptation to evaluate one as superior and the other as inferior disappears completely. Then sometimes Marie's hands go like that and Vimala's hands go like this. So the relationship to the conditionings undergoes a radical change. It loses its grip on you. It loses the capacity to distort and twist your relationship with love. It is just there.

Like dead ashes, the conditionings are there because the content of the human consciousness cannot be wiped out, just as the color of the skin cannot be washed out. They are there. But once you see false as false, that is the beginning of seeing the truth as the truth. To see the conditionings for what they are is already going beyond them: otherwise, you wouldn't see them as conditionings. So they remain there, harmless, unaggressive, and noninterfering, and the hangover of those conditionings may get reflected in involuntary reflexes and involuntary actions. But on the plane of volition, the conditionings have no control, and in the realm of spontaneity of relationship they cannot interfere. So they no longer constitute bondage. If you could wipe out all knowledge, if you could wipe out all memory—memory as a faculty and memory as a capacity developed through centuries—then you would take human beings regressively back to the animal level. Antirationalism, anticerebralism, is a very reactionary activity. The human race has worked very hard in developing reason, the brain, the symbols, the languages, and now human beings see the limitations of all that. But if you deny all that, if you want to destroy all that, if you try to negate it, then I think that you take away the beauty and the elegance of the brain: the competence, the efficiency, and the rich inheritance. Why should the inheritance be a bondage? Why? It is not bondage unless you are attached to it, unless you want to impose it upon others. It is the ambition to impose upon others that constitutes bondage, not the inheritance, not the culture. To see the conditioning as conditioning takes away the arrogance to assert, to become aggressive, to impose, to force things on others; it eliminates the arrogance, the ambition to convert others to your point of view, and there remains the gesture of friendship—communication, exchange, reciprocity, mutuality, learning from one another—and I, for one, would not settle for anything else. So to see the conditioning as conditioning is a great event that takes the sting out of the conditioning, so that no more sting is left.

CHAPTER EIGHT

Patterns of Self-Deception

Mount Abu; July 21, 1973

As long as man does not get acquainted with the invisible cerebral organ, as long as he does not understand the mechanism of mind, it is nearly impossible to arrive at the state of meditation.

Man has discovered by now, in the East as well as the West, that the physical body, the human body, the biological organism, is the same the world over. The bone structure may differ slightly and the color of the skin may differ slightly, but the modus operandi of the biological organism is one and the same. The appetite or the power of digestion may differ slightly. In the same way, the functions of the human body—performed by the lungs, the heart, the kidney, the liver, the optical nerves, and the auditory nerves—are the same the world over. That is why doctors of one country can operate upon patients of another country. The biological organism has a universal way of functioning. It is governed by universal laws that are neither Western nor Eastern. There are neither Hindu laws of digestion nor Christian laws of kidney operation; there are neither Muslim laws for the eyes to function nor Buddhist laws for the ears to function. The complex biological mechanism functions in a universal way.

It is an illusion to say that the body belongs to you; that it is owned by you; that you can do anything with it; that you can treat it as you like, feed it as you like, and put it to sleep when you like; and at the same time hope that the biological organism will cooperate with you: that it will be alert, healthy, subtle, and fresh. The body has a certain way of operation, and has to be taken care of in that way. There are universal laws of health, and the body has an organic relationship with the universe existing outside the skin.

The body has a relationship with the sunshine; it has a relationship with the clouds and the rain; and it has a relationship with the earth, the water, and the breeze. The five elements existing outside the human body and the five elements existing inside the human body have an organic relationship with one another. One has to get acquainted with the nature of the organic relationship and find a harmonious way of sustaining it. The moment that the relationship is snapped, the moment that there is a gap between the inner and the outer, the body is indisposed. If the balance between the water, the earth, and the fire contained in the body is disturbed, then the body is in disease. You know what disease is: dis-ease, disharmony. To say that you own the body and you can do anything with it is only an expression of ignorance.

In the same way, there is a psychological structure that you call the mind, that you call the brain, that you call the cerebral organ. You cannot ordinarily see it with your eyes, but it is located in the head. It is much more complex than the other parts of the body. This sense organ called the brain is a very complex, a very delicate, and a highly strung instrument. One has to get acquainted with it. The ways of the mind are the same the world over. To think, to feel, to formulate ideas and ideologies, and to construct ways of behavior and patterns of behavior: all this is done by the mind the world over. The way man deals with anger, jealousy, grief, and violence is the same the world over. Anger is one cerebral way of behavior; jealousy is another cerebral way. Just as the rest of the body has a way of operating, so, too, the brain has a way of operating. It receives an impression, interprets it, and reacts to it. Patterns of reactions are different, just as the patterns of cooking meals and putting on clothes and building a house are different. A Japanese house is not like a Dutch house; Dutch houses are not like Norwegian houses. The Dutch have found a way to manipulate space and to build a house. The Japanese have another way. In the same way, the patterns of reaction may be different. But the raw materials with which the patterns have been constructed are the same. The desire to dominate, to own, to possess, to aspire, to compete, to compare: all these are universal ways of the human mind.

When a person looks upon anger as his anger and jealousy as his jealousy, he unnecessarily creates a problem out of a simple cerebral way of behavior. When he looks upon thoughts as his possession and says, "These are my thoughts, my values, my norms, and my criteria," he creates a relationship of ownership and possession with the cerebral organ. Just as you cannot deal with the body according to your whims and wishes, but must be acquainted with it, understand it, and cooperate with it, in the same way, you have to cooperate with the psychological structure. So a spiritual inquiry has to begin with this very clear and lucid understanding that the mind never belongs to an individual. Your mind is but one expression of the universal mind. Your mind is an expression of the global human mind. It cannot be owned or possessed by you. It cannot be treated the way your sweet desire would like to treat it. It is the maltreatment of the mind that creates a problem; it is ignorance about the mechanism of the mind that creates a problem.

Before we talk about silence getting transformed into meditation, one must be very clear that this mind as it is, the mind that is inherited by man today, has certain ways of operation, certain channels through which it functions. It has certain symbols through which it recognizes the world outside and inside. It has its own language, and it interprets life in terms of this language. All this is built in within you. You cannot wish away the mind. You cannot turn away from the mind. You cannot destroy the mind. Thus the content of the human mind is the racial human knowledge and experience. That is the content of human consciousness. That is the content of the human psyche.

During your life of twenty years, or forty, fifty, or eighty years, some patterns of behavior have been acquired by you, some have been inherited from your family, some have been inherited from your community, and some have been inherited from the whole human race. They are all there. They are very compact in a very subtle, condensed form, and they make their existence felt when you are awake and moving in relationship. While you are sleeping, the content of the consciousness makes itself felt through dreams, through visions, through intimations, through urges, and through blind passions that are related to your reason, your logic, your knowledge—or to nothing at all. So all this is there. It is a vast area that has been covered by human effort throughout the centuries. So one would suggest to the inquirers that they get acquainted with the particular way that their mind functions. The mind being a particular expression of the universal, or the racial, mind, let the inquirer investigate it, examine it personally, not theoretically, but personally in daily life, let him find out what his mind is like and how it functions.

When you want to look at yourself, you stand before the mirror. And then you notice that you are too thin or too fat or not well proportioned or pale, whatever it is, but you have to stand before the mirror to look at yourself. You get reflected as you are into the mirror. People may tell you that you look like this or you look like that, but to have a personal encounter with yourself, a firsthand personal discovery, you have to stand before the mirror and look at yourself. Only then do you notice any visible deformity or disability or weakness or distortion. To notice the distortion personally, to discover it personally, you have to look at yourself: a thousand persons may tell you, but you won't find it; unless you look at yourself, you won't understand it or its particular location. In the same way, you have to find out how the mind is and that just as the body gets reflected into the mirror, so, too, the mind gets reflected in your behavior from morning till night.

Relationships are the mirror into which your inner being gets reflected as it is. This is true unless you have become too sophisticated to talk and behave freely and spontaneously, and you always adhere to the rules of etiquette, politeness, and culture, to the oughts and ought nots, musts and must nots. If you do that, then your behavior is under pressure. Pressurized behavior cannot reflect the quality of your inner behavior: it distorts, it creates a wrong impression. It gives you a wrong impression about yourself. It creates a wrong image in your mind of yourself. But there are moments and there are relationships when you are not on the defensive, when you are frank, when you feel free to be what you are, perhaps with your spouse, with your children, with your intimate friends, or when you are alone. Just as climbing the Himalayas has to begin with the first step where you stand at the foot of the hill, the noncerebral voyage into the dimension of silence and meditation has to begin with the personal discovery of the mind as it is, as it exists in you, and as it expresses itself in you and through you. That would be the first step. To take a journey of a thousand miles, you have to begin with the first step from the place where you stand. The romantic description of the journey and the things that the body sees on the way and the description of the scenery are of no use unless you lift your foot and take the first step.

The voyage, the journey, has to begin. And so the first step is, *Let me examine the quality of my mind: the shoddiness, the shabbiness, the poverty, the richness, the stupidity or the intelligence, the ignorance or the learnedness, the scholarship; let me see.* A personal examination of the ways of psychological behavior in daily relationships is absolutely necessary. But the friend may say, "I do not know how to look at myself, because when I am talking, when I am responding to situations, I cannot observe. I cannot do both things, respond to the situation and look at myself. How can I do these two things together?" If you experiment with this for a day or two, then you will notice how this personal examination and observation of the behavior is difficult, as we have not been educated to do that. How you move your hands, feet, neck, or eyes, when you look at people, when you are alone, when you get up, when you eat, when you drink, what you feel when you are engaged in one of these activities, you have never observed yourself, and so you do not understand: that is the daily contradiction in the life of an inquirer. He presumes that the mind as it is, the quality of the mind that he has, is capable of finding God or divinity. If a person is lame, then he has the honesty and the humility to say, *I cannot climb.* But those who are psychologically lame have never learned to think, to feel, and to do things out of their own spontaneity; instead, they have been doing things out of compulsion, and have been floating on social customs, traditions, rituals. When they begin to inquire for themselves, they think they can capture reality in the grip of their tiny, shoddy, arrogant minds. All those who wander around in search of techniques and methods, and all those who wander around promising them methods and techniques, together create an illusion that the human mind as it is can capture divinity or God: the totality of existence.

This illusion has caused many an inquirer to spend his whole life searching, and in the evening of his life to say, "I tried my level best, but I could not get it. I listened to the talks, I went through the rituals, and I followed that practice. I did this under the illusion that the I and the structure around the I, were a vehicle with which I was going to get it." None of you would think of experimenting with a spaceship tomorrow without training, without education; none of you would say, *If that fellow could go to the moon, I will also go to the moon*—without taking any education about the spaceship, how you will have to live in the change of the atmosphere, and so on. So, you know, it requires some education. So it is an illusion that the human mind as it is—cultured, sophisticated, civilized—can capture the dimension of meditation, own it, possess it as an experience, and can capture God, the divinity, the immeasurable, the unnameable in the framework of man's own experience. This illusion has to go. Unless we purge our minds of this illusion, the next step cannot be taken. We may talk, discuss, thrash out the issues as citizens, but academic discussions or verbal speculations these days do not help when it comes to actual living.

So by examining the mechanism of the mind, the quality of the mind, the ways of the mind's functioning in your daily relationships, you will discover the limitations of the cerebral organ that you have. You will discover the frontiers of the mind. You will discover, for example, that when you feel joy in moments of communion with nature or with other individuals, that joy cannot be expressed in words. You will discover how love cannot be touched by words or languages or patterns of behavior; you will discover that freedom cannot be touched by the mind; and you will discover that the mind can acquire information, organize it, and convert it into knowledge. The mind can acquire knowledge, but acquiring knowledge does not result in understanding. So one sees the limitations of the mind: the capacity to acquire information, the capacity to organize it skillfully, and the capacity to handle it skillfully do not add up to understanding. One has to see this. When you discover that you tell a lie ten times a day or four times a week, you see for yourself how you tell a lie, how some motive makes you tell a lie; how telling a lie, or falsehood, makes you afraid; and how that fear inhibits your relationships. You see all this in operation. You discover that knowing the truth does not enable you to live the truth. There is, in fact, a difference between knowledge and understanding.

And this is not an academic difference: this is a difference that gets expressed when you move in relationship. Ordinarily, you feel that you know the truth and you speak the truth and you are a very truthful person. You have an image of yourself. Part of the image you have of yourself is that you do not get angry, you are not easily irritable. You have this image because whenever anger surges up, you push it away and cover it up. And you won't look at it. But anger does not disappear because you do not look at it. It is still there, pushed under a cover or tucked up neatly behind etiquette, behind a polite gesture, or behind the effort to suppress it. It is there. Unless you examine your behavior, how anger surges up and how you suppress it and push it into the background, your image that you are a person who never gets angry will remain intact. You will have this false image of yourself unless you personally examine your behavior, understand the motivational forces behind your behavior, and understand the limitations of the mind, of the brain. This is absolutely necessary. Personal observation of the quality of behavior is absolutely necessary, and for this you do not need any experts to help you. Do it for the fun of it, for a week or for a couple of days. There is a gap between your motive and the verbal expression of the motive. Just watch the gap: you have a motive and you feel ashamed to confess this motive even to yourself, and you want to hide this motive from others. You clothe the motive in different ways: this forms the gap between the actual nature of the motive—the motive force, the intention, the purpose, the ambition—and the verbal expression that you give to it. "I intend to do this": that is what you say. But when you say "I intend to do this," you may mean an absolutely different thing. Maybe the verbal expression and the motive are in contradiction with each other. They are incompatible. But you create a world of make-believe: you believe that really you do not want that. Somewhere inside, you see that you want it, but you make yourself believe that you do not want it and you behave in a third way.

So there is a gap between the actual motive and the verbal clothing that you have put upon the motive to impress upon yourself that you do not want this and instead you want that. Then the scarecrow—the verbal expression—again deceives when you move into relationship or your efforts to hide the motive prove fruitless and other individuals find out your motive because the momentum of the motive is too much for your verbal concealing and hiding. It speaks through your eyes, it speaks through the tone of your words, it speaks through the gestures of your whole body. It is great fun to watch the whole game that man plays with himself. So there is a gap between the actual motive, the verbal expression of the motive, and the nature of the action. Find out whether they are mutually compatible or contradictory, and how, within yourself, you get torn half a dozen times a day.

And this world of make-believe goes on flourishing: every day you create a world of make-believe around yourself. It is a very expensive self-deception. It is only your habit of self-deception that creates and sustains this false image of yourself. I carry my image of myself and you carry your image of yourself. Those images meet, they come into conflict, and the relationship gets strained. So when you begin to examine the quality of your mind as it gets expressed in actual relationships, you will discover that to relate to the other person, to the other individual, is extremely difficult, because you are not related to yourself.

Your motives and your actions are strangers to each other: there is no relationship. So there is a gap. And if there is a relationship, it is a strained relationship, and therefore, at the end of the day, you are tired. You get tired because you have to deal with so many relationships: as a husband, as a wife, as a shopkeeper, as a businessman, as a boss, as a secretary, as a typist, as a citizen of society, as a member of the community, you have to deal with an innumerable variety of relationships. And in every relationship, this gap between the motive, the words, and the action—the contradiction among these things—eats into your vitality. Instead of giving you vitality, these relationships exhaust you completely. You are a person torn within yourself, fragmented and divided within yourself, but you have to move out of your skin through words and gestures and go on doing your job in life. So it is the division and fragmentation within that exhaust you, and not your relationships.

To live is to be related. Life is relationship, but these relationships exhaust you because you are divided, fragmented, in contradiction, in conflict, in constant tension, within yourself. That is what the personal discovery brings to your notice. You also observe that whenever there is no gap between the motive, the verbal expression, and the action, there is great joy. When these three function not as an artificially integrated whole, but as a homogeneous whole, then you feel joy, then you are relaxed, then you move freely, and relationship does not tire you, does not exhaust you.

An inquirer has to discover the science and the art of moving through relationship without friction, without inner contradiction, without tension. Only then can the last cerebral voyage take place, because you have to eat when you are hungry, you have to have a roof over your head, and you have to live among other people. If the spiritual inquiry takes you away from other human beings and into isolation, then the very isolation will inhibit the inquiry. The essence of freedom cannot be found when you are alone. Freedom can breathe and vibrate only when you are with other people; if you are not with other people, freedom has no meaning, and love has no meaning, because the essence of life, love, truth, freedom, and silence express themselves only when you are in relationship. Therefore, before we talk about silence and meditation, will it not be helpful to all of us as sober and sincere inquirers who have gathered together in such a small number in an intimate atmosphere of friendship, to examine not only the quality of the mind, and the quality of thoughts, feelings, sentiments, but the actual movement of the mind in operation.

When you stand before a mirror and the mirror shows unto you that you are not handsome, that you are ugly, or that you are not tall or are very tall or are very short, when the mirror shows you that, do you get angry with the mirror? You stand at the shores of a very beautiful, serene lake and you look into it and you see your reflection. Do you get angry with the reflection or with yourself? You only find out that something has got to be done about it. The body seems to have gotten out of control: something will have to be done. That is all you say. But when you notice the different parts of the body and their qualities and their relationships with one another, do you throw away the mirror because it shows that you are ugly, that you are not clean, or that the body is swollen?

In the same way, when you begin to observe how you behave in relationships and the relationships show you that you are a barbarian, you have an element of savageness, you are greedy, you are filled with contradictions, do you become depressed? Do you become frustrated? Do you feel that you must throw away the mind, that others have very good minds and you don't? When you compare yourself with other people, are you jealous that you are more violent than one person and less alert than another person, comparing and contrasting yourself with your superiors and your inferiors? Just as you do not throw away the mirror because it shows you the fact of your physical existence, you do not give up relationships because they cause you to express your inner life. You do not turn away from relationships because they show distortion. So while living with people and going through relationships, the inner voyage has to be launched. And I hope that you will not forget what we spoke of earlier: the mind has universal ways of functioning and operating. The cerebral ways, or patterns of behavior, are not your personal property; they are not your personal monopoly. Whether you are a Hindu, a Christian, or a Muslim, this is the way that your mind functions.

And when this clarity of understanding is there, then the exposure of your inner contradictions and complexities does not lead to frustration or self-pity. You are not looking at your inner life and its expression in order to change it, mind you: you are not looking at it so that you can transform it, convert it. It has a momentum of thousands of years behind it. It has a momentum of the whole human race behind it. You cannot change it overnight or even in ten years or fifteen years. You can patch it up: a slight reform here and a mild reform there. That can happen. But you cannot transform the whole material. The mind is as it is. When there is no desire to change what is, then the exposure does not cause self-pity or depression or frustration. Only an ambitious mind wants to look at itself in order to change itself. An ambitious mind feels frustrated, because even while observing, it is comparing itself with others. It's an old habit: comparing, evaluating. We shall proceed further with this issue when we meet next.

CHAPTER NINE

Peace Beyond Compare

International Youth Talk
Mount Abu; July 22, 1973

There seems to be a built-in yearning, a craving, in each human heart for a state of joy that will not be affected by the behavior of other people. There is a dream, a vision, in every human heart of a state of love. This state cannot be emulated by the game of attachment, jealousy, envy, or the game of withdrawal and detachment. The vision of a state of love, the vision of a state of peace and of joy, seems to me to be built into the human heart. Yet man, who has inhabited the globe for millions of years, has not realized the vision, has not arrived at a state of joy, unpoisoned by pleasure and pain, the state of peace undisturbed by the relationship through which one has to go, the state of love which is impregnable and has neither diminished nor increased with changes in the surroundings. So those who force the mind have not arrived at this state, though they have an unarticulated, a nonverbalized, yearning for peace, love, friendship, and joy.

In spite of all the propaganda of organized religion, innumerable techniques and methods of pacifying the mind, soothing the brain, you and I as human beings feel unfulfilled. You can acquire all the assets that you are capable of and the society in which you live can offer you. You may acquire property, social recognition, and political and economic power; you may acquire psychic power and psychological power; and yet all these acquisitions leave the heart cold and empty. You may become a learned scholar; you may learn pranayama and yoga, and become a hatha yogi;

you may learn the methods of tantra and become a tantric and a mantric, specializing in tantras and mantras. But the acquisition of physical, psychological, or psychic power does not necessarily enable you to feel fulfilled, to live in a state of peace, happiness, joy, or love.

Why is this? Could it be that the road to acquisition, ownership, possession, the road to becoming something, is not the road to fulfillment at all? I wonder if you have ever experienced harmony. How is a well dug? We had to dig wells when we were working in Bhudan with the Land Gift Movement, day by day digging the earth, removing the rocks, the boulders: working together. I have worked with Vinoba [Vinoba Bhave], digging a well. It is a very interesting experience. When you dig a well, as you dig, you remove the earth, the pieces of rock, the roots of trees, and the boulders. You have not acquired anything while you are digging. And when you have dug deeply enough, suddenly you come across a stream of water, a living, bubbling, crystal clear spring of water. You could say that your digging has created a stream of water. If you had not dug, you would not have come across, you would not be able to touch, the living waters of the spring. But you can academically discover how deep you have to dig, and with what instruments you have to dig, and how many hours of manpower you have to put in. You may discuss all these aspects of the job, but if you sit there without digging, you will never come across fresh water, you will not be able to touch it, or drink and quench your thirst. The digging has not created the spring of water. The spring has always been there. Your digging is not the cause that has brought about the effect. The spring was there. But it was invisible, intangible. You could not touch it. You could not do it properly. You have not created it. You have not obtained it. Perhaps the process of becoming or acquiring, the process of experiencing, takes you in the opposite direction of peace, joy, and love.

When you climb a hill or a mountain, step by step, very cautiously, then your body, according to the altitude and according to the nature of the soil and the rocks, gets the feel of the rock formation, and your feet are in close contact with the mountain in the climbing. The horizons go on widening. There is more space around you and more sunshine; the air is clearer and purer than in the valley. But you have not acquired anything. The mountain path was there waiting for you to travel over it, but you have not acquired anything. You have not become something different from what you were when you were standing at the foot of the hill. You have made certain movements and taken certain actions, and certain inner changes have taken place. Your metabolism responds to your action of climbing. The deep breathing that you naturally go through, the conservation of energy that is required to climb a rock, gives you the feeling of living every moment alertly, sensitively. You do not climb to acquire anything, but for the joy of climbing.

When you take a plunge into a pool, a lake, a river, or the sea and swim, the thing that you learn, or experience, is the intimate contact of the waves with your body. The salty waters of the sea or the ocean stimulate the heat in your body. So many changes take place. You come out of the water, and what have you acquired?

Man, whether in the name of religion or spirituality, or in the name of holy life, is possessed with the idea of acquisition, ownership, possession, becoming, and comparing himself with others. So he never arrives at the source of joy, love, and peace within himself. It is always an outward activity, never an inward activity. It is always an outward voyage, never an inward voyage. When you get acquainted with the physical body, you do away with the secondary, unessential, or unnecessary things. It is like conditioning. You are acquainted with the mind and the speech. You examine them with intensity, and understanding the mind and the body removes a lot of dirt from your life when you see things for what they are, without justifying them, without defending them, without fighting against them. Then those conditionings of love lie there within the structure, harmless, a spent force, having no grip whatsoever. That is like removing the rocks of the earth.

Understanding removes the dirt of inaccuracy, imprecision, ignorance, distortion, and twistings, and if that is done, you feel yourself in an atmosphere of clarity, lucidity; you feel light. Understanding enlightens you. You know the meaning of the word *enlightenment*: that which throws light on the object of your perception, audition, or relationship; that which throws light on yourself. It is only the understanding that enlightens you. Enlightenment is not something mysterious, not something mystical: when you clearly see things as they are and understand their relationship with the whole of your life, your life gets enlightened. It gets flooded with the light of your understanding. You are no more in a state of self-deception and therefore, no more capable of cheating and deceiving others. You see the false as the false. You see the crooked as the crooked, without going into an analysis, comparing the causes, or defending, justifying, or explaining them.

And the simplicity and humility of a person of understanding enables him to be what he is: a person who moves through life with no desire to compare himself with others, to become something different from what he is, to acquire something psychologically or psychically, or to own, to possess. The more you go through experiences, the more conditioned you get. Unless you are eager to become something other than what you are, you will not run after experiences.

Experience mongering, pleasure mongering: they are both conditioned. To be in the dimension, to live in the is-ness of your own being, is to be at peace with your own being. But when you compare yourself with someone else or something else, your peace is disturbed. If you can move in relationship without comparing yourself with others, your peace will never be damaged.

If you reconcile yourself with what you are, then there will be no desire to impose yourself upon others, there will be no aggression, verbal renunciation; there will be communication, there will be communion, there will be living together. But living together does not take place because all the time you are comparing yourself with others, evaluating, judging, trying to become what you are not, pretending to be what you are not, hiding from what you are. This whole business keeps you in isolation. There is no living together. The way to fulfillment, the way to joy, the way to peace and love, is to come face-to-face with what you are: the limitations, the conditionings, the tendencies, the weaknesses, to see them as what they are, to see the frontiers of physical strength as well as mental strength, to see the limitations of the physical structure as well as the cerebral structure, to use the structures whenever it is necessary and to relax in the nonuse of those structures, to relax in the state of silence, in the state of is-ness, whenever the movement of the physical or cerebral structure is unwarranted; to use these structures only when it is necessary and otherwise to relax in the is-ness.

To relax in the is-ness of your life is to be at peace. Peace is not different from this. When you relax into what you are, aware of the limitations of the brain and the mind, aware of the nature of the conditionings of the brain and the body, capable of using the brain whenever it is necessary, you relax because you have nothing to hide, nothing to pretend, nothing to show off, and nothing to suppress. It is only when you compare that this whole business of suppression and depression comes about. So you relax in your own is-ness. That relaxation is joy. Such a person goes through pleasure and pain. The pleasure may stimulate the face slightly, and the pain may cause a shrinking of facial or other nerves. But he experiences the smile on the lips or the shrinking of the nerves in a relaxed way, not trying to seek one and avoid the other, not running after one and running away from the other. Giving up or acquiring is not the way to feel fulfilled in life. That is not the way to love and joy.

I hope that you will not misunderstand. You have to have a livelihood, you have to take a job, you have to provide yourself and the members of your family with food, shelter, clothing, and so on. I am not talking about that. That has to be done. But when there is no desire and ambition to become richer than your neighbor, to become more powerful than Tom, Dick, and Harry, to have more recognition and prestige than other relatives and friends, then simply having a job and earning a livelihood becomes an inevitable thing. Otherwise, the temptation to compare and compete brings about complications in your economic life.

CHAPTER TEN

The Observer and the Observed

Mount Abu; July 23, 1973

Between the object of perception or the object of audition and yourself, at first there is just your seeing or your hearing. If you are interested in an object, then from seeing, the attention gets limited to a particular object, and seeing becomes looking. From looking you go into observing. That is to say, you begin to take notice, you begin to get interested. You see many things. You look at one thing, you get interested in it either out of some motive or due to the nature of the object of perception, and you look at it. Out of that looking, you go into observing. Observation does not last, is not sustained, and you proceed to recognize it, to recognize the object as distinct from the other, its name, its species, its kind, its quality, its nature, and so on: you recognize it. Recognizing implies identifying and putting the object into a category. That is recognition. But if you don't stop there, then the activity goes on, and you begin to compare: I like this more than the other; I do not like this; I want it, I do not want it; this is bad, this is good. A comparative evaluation takes place. So you go from seeing to looking, from looking to observing, from observing to recognizing, from recognizing to comparing and evaluating. You arrive at a judgment about the object, and you interpret that judgment in relation to the other aspects of your life. All this goes on very quickly in yourself. So you have to see very clearly the differences between the seeing, looking, observing, recognizing, judging, and interpreting: different shapes of mental activity. And with most of us, the state of observation is not sustained. To observe means to look at something without wanting anything in return, without comparing the object with the past or with the present, without evaluating it, without judging it; thus we cannot remain quietly in the state of observation.

We have the capacity, but yet that capacity has been neglected, just as so many other capacities of the human mind have been neglected: this capability, this innate capability in man of looking at a thing innocently. We are capable of it, potentially. You see children looking innocently at a rainbow, at a cloud, at raindrops, at a sparrow, at a parrot, or at flowers. The child looks at the thing with his whole body, not only with his eyes, but as if the whole universe were condensed into that flower, into that bud, and so on. So there is in childhood the capacity to look at a thing innocently without wanting anything from that object, or, for that matter, without wanting anything from that individual. The child can look at it. The beauty of that innocence begins to fade away when the child goes to school, begins to move out into society, into the community, and if the child is looking at certain things, we elders say, "Don't stare at it: it is bad; it is not done; don't look at that. When you sit with other people, don't look at them, don't stare at them. Other people are close by: don't stare at those people." We call it "staring." What I want to say is this: there is a potentiality to sustain the innocent look, the innocent gaze.

When you sustain that, when that is sustained, that is the state of observation. Most of us are not yet capable of that. So when an inquirer asks where you begin, how you set about it, one likes to suggest that you learn to observe once again, you relearn how to observe. Sit quietly with yourself, observing the physical movements, the verbal movements, and the mental movements; sit down with yourself quietly. So sitting in silence, or sitting in quietness by yourself, is the way to learn to sustain the state of observation. Unless that is sustained, you cannot observe yourself and the quality of your behavior, the nature of your motivational forces, the texture of your relationships throughout the day. So one suggests that if you are to learn this, then you spend some time with yourself.

When you learn to observe, without analyzing, without interpreting, without arriving at a judgment, you find out that it is not easy: it is more easily said than done. Because as you begin to observe, suddenly likes and dislikes come up, values come up, judgment comes up, and deeply rooted habits come up. So you return to observing, and before you know it, the state of observation lapses into the state of analysis, interpretation, evaluation, judgment, and so on. Once again, you become aware of it and again observe; and once again, the state of observation lapses into the state of interpretation. That is to say, you grow into the capacity to become aware that you are not observing. For some time you observe and then for some time you are not in the state of observation. But you learn to become aware of the state of nonobservation. That is a sensitivity into which you grow. So if a person does not condemn himself and say, "I cannot sit, because the moment I begin to observe, the thoughts, the evaluations, the values, and the comparisons come up." It does not matter: let them come. They are there. Therefore, they get exposed. If you do not run away, and if you are satisfied with the awareness of the inattention of the nonobservation, then the sensitivity, the intensity, and the duration of observation go on increasing. When that is sustained, observation has a steady state of consciousness: please do see this noncomparative, noninterpreting attention. Observation is noncomparative, nonevaluating, and noninterpretive attention.

When that is sustained, then in daily relationships you act and you are aware of why you are acting in such a way. You see the reaction of the other person and how you react to his reaction to you, and you know the whole thing. So you have to correlate the two. You have to go into it. When you wish to learn how to observe, you have to correlate these two, that is to say, work on both fronts. You have to work with yourself, upon yourself, in the quietness of your room whenever you have the leisure, and you have to be aware in your daily relations.

So observation in relationships and observation in solitude: they go hand in hand. Now, are they the same? Are they similar? In one way, yes, and in another way, no. In one way, they are similar because the quality of consciousness when observation is sustained is the same. Whether you observe yourself sitting alone or whether you observe yourself in relationships, the state of observation makes your consciousness very alert, very sharp, and very quick. So whether you do it in solitude while you are sitting in silence or you do it in relationships, the quality of your consciousness goes on changing. The quality of consciousness—the quickness, the sharpness, the alertness, the sensitivity—they are the logical results of both.

In another way, observation in solitude and observation in relationships are different, because when I sit by myself in silence and observe, I have the security that there is no one else in the room who will see what is going on within myself. When my stupidity, when my shoddiness, my shabbiness, my cruelty, my violence, and so on, get exposed to me in the solitude of my own room, which is locked from within, I feel the security that there is no one else who knows it. There is no one else before whom or to whom this inner state gets exposed. When I am in daily relationships, there, too, I am in the state of observation. Supposing that I feel jealous and my jealousy gets expressed while I am with certain individuals. I am talking to them and working with them, and I feel jealous. Now I feel jealous while with them and I am aware that I feel jealous. And this awareness of my own jealousy makes me a bit uncomfortable.

Human beings do not really like to be dishonest, and they do not really like to be violent or angry. That is not in their reach. Other considerations—social, economic, and political factors—have taught man to tolerate his own savageness and even to glorify it, but when you take the human individual from the East or the West, from whichever country you like, he does not like all that. There is inner goodness in man, there is potential divinity in man. That is why the human race has a future. So while in relationships, I feel angry and I am aware that I am angry and because I am aware of that anger and my state of getting angry, I would like to see that the other individual does not notice my anger or at least does not notice that I am aware of my anger. You see the complexity! So I feel a bit uncomfortable to be in the state of observation. In this discomfort, I feel a bit embarrassed, and in this state of embarrassment, I want to hide from the other person.

So to sustain observation while you are with people—living with them, moving with them, and working with them—you need tremendous humility and a very intense inquiry. So I can say to myself, *It does not matter if the other person notices that I am angry and that I am aware that I am angry; it does not matter if his image of me is shattered.* You know, as long as I am angry and I pretend that I am not angry, I put up an image with great effort before other people that I feel safe and secure, but the state of observation makes it impossible for me to deceive myself. Self-deception and the state of observation are mutually incompatible. So people say, well, it is better to sit in silence in a room and observe and then analyze according to Freud, Jung, Adler, Martin, depth psychology, Pavlov, and so on. But when you are sitting and observing alone, justifications can come up, defenses can come up. When you are with people, there is no time for self-defense, for justification, for explanation, or for referring to theories. You are face-to-face with the other person, with your anger and your awareness of the anger, do you see? That is why it is hard work. It is arduous work and needs tremendous energy and humility to sustain observation, to see yourself as you are, and because you see yourself as you are, you make no effort to project a different image for the other person.

That is the only austerity that is required of an inquirer: the austerity of humility to see things as they are, to see my inner being as it is when it gets reflected in relationships, to observe it as it is, without defending it, without justifying it, without interpreting it, and without relegating the responsibility of those states to other people. I could easily say that my inheritance is responsible. I could easily say that society is responsible. Very easily, I could say the responsibility belongs to the schools, the teachers, and the leaders. I could delegate all the responsibility, scatter it all over society, and feel, *Poor me: I was helpless.* The anger, the jealousy, the greed, and the violence are due to 1, 2, 3, 4. I could count more factors—and feel that I am not responsible. It might seem that delegating the responsibility to others, putting the blame upon others, would not hurt me so much. But what does it actually do to me? When I delegate the responsibility and put the blame upon other people and feel, *Poor me: I am the victim, I am helpless,* then I enter into such a deep pit of self-pity that no one else could pull me out of that pit of self-pity. It is a valley into which I go rolling down every time that I notice a shortcoming: I put the blame upon someone else and make others responsible.

I do not deny the theories of Freud, or Jung, or any of the psychologists. I have no quarrel with any of the psychologists. But what I would like to suggest is this: when you observe, you see the inner life, the good or the bad. If you see the good and feel elated and proud that these are your qualities, these are your virtues, and try to become a proprietor of those virtues, those good qualities, then again you get isolated. And if you see the defects, the mistakes, or the shortcomings, and you delegate the responsibility and put the blame upon others, then you enter into self-pity. Self-pity isolates you as much as pride and vanity isolate you. Either way you are isolated. So it requires tremendous energy, and you know humility is the eternal fountain of energy. I have one foot at that fountain. As a friend, I say to you that humility is the perennial source of energy, or freshness. Humility enables you to learn, keeps you pliable, perhaps till the last breath: I hope so. Pride, vanity, and arrogance have no momentum: they are sterile, and they get exhausted and they exhaust you so very quickly.

So one says I am out to understand the meaning of life, I would like to see the divine, the real, God, however I term it, within me and around me, so let me see things as they are. Observation in actual relationships escalates the speed much more than observation done in the security of a room, because the challenges are not so intimate there and there is a temptation to go into abstraction, academic abstraction, when you observe, because there you are observing the past or you are observing an idea of anger, an idea of a sexual urge, or an idea of violence. But when you are face-to-face with violence, it is bubbling, it is coming up within you, living, vibrating, affecting your nerves, your mind, your speech, everything. You are face-to-face with anger with the people around you and with the awareness, the state of observation, of that anger. Oh, such a thrill! So you may feel embarrassed and yet you don't want to hide, you don't want to wear your heart on your sleeve and say, *Oh, wait a minute, brother, I have a feeling of anger, I am in the state of observation of anger.* You don't verbalize that. You don't say all those things, and you don't get sentimental or excited about it, because you have to live with that person or you have to work with that person. You have to drive a car, post a letter, or do the shopping: all sorts of things need to be done. So you may get embarrassed, go through the embarrassment, and do the thing necessary without waiting to see the other person's reaction to your embarrassment, the impact of your reaction upon the person.

So I am moving to another point. Now you are not much concerned with the reaction of the other person. If you don't value yourself according to the reactions of other people, you don't want to weigh yourself in their eyes, then it is easy to live in humility and easy to sustain the state of observation. If you are terribly concerned about what the other person will think about you, what he will say about you, what he will feel about you, what he will tell other people about you, if you are terribly concerned about what other people have got to say about you and will say about you, then observation can never take place. So the challenges are more intimate, the situation is more complex, and more humility and austerity of inquiry are needed. But all these put together make you so tense and they escalate the speed so much that the texture of relationships goes through a change in a very short time.

[At this point, Vimala responds to a participant's question.]

This is a very interesting question: "Are you saying that when there is anger, the anger does not allow observation?" Look, I am learning how to observe; observation as a dimension of my consciousness is not there. What I have been brought up to do as a human being is to look at things with a motive; to accept them psychologically, to reject them psychologically, to acquire them psychologically or physically, or to reject them, to call them good or bad, and to judge them thus. That is what I have been taught to do. And now here is an inquirer who understands that from interpretation, analysis, and evaluation, he has to go back to the state of observation and sustain that bare, simple attention, noninterpretive and noncomparative attention. Then only the observed and the observer can go into abeyance. When he realizes this, he is learning how to observe, whether sitting in his room alone or in relationship.

Once an inquirer has grown into the state of observation, whether in waking hours or in sleeping hours, the consciousness inhales and exhales only observation. Then the question of anger or violence does not come up. But we are talking about the state of inquiry when the inquirer is learning to observe, whether he is alone in his room sitting in silence or learning to observe in daily relationship. We are not talking about the state of observation as a dimension coming to life, in which the inquirer lives all the time. We are talking about an inquirer learning how to observe and grow into that dimension. These are two different stages.

But let me say one thing. The anger, the violence, or whatever it is, the greed, the jealousy, or the temptation to tell a lie, will arise naturally, if you don't affect the body or the mind with any chemicals, drugs, if you do not affect the brain cells and the chemical condition of the body with mantras, chakras, or tantras. If you do not inhibit the body and the brain cells, then all these cerebral ways of behavior are bound to get stimulated by the brain and their existence can be felt. If you do not numb yourself—it is becoming very popular to numb the mind, to numb brain cells, or to stimulate them to such an intensity, heighten their sensitivity in such a short period that abruptly you find yourself beyond the senses, in a different world—if you neither inhibit nor stimulate, if you do not suppress, deny, negate, or worship it through so-called devotion and other emotional and sentimental things, if you do none of this, then the whole conditioned human mind, the total human consciousness that you and I have inherited, vibrates with every challenge. It is a condition. So it gets stimulated in every relationship. So people say, *Let us see that it does not get stimulated,* but I would like to suggest that you do not numb it, chill it down, affect it artificially with drugs, but simply understand it and feel that it is there.

So understanding purifies. Not knowledge. Knowledge never purifies a person. Nor does it have any dynamism. It is sterile. Because it is information gathered from books or individuals and organized, put into order, but still it is something acquired intellectually, it can become your intellectual property. It can decorate your brain. But it does not percolate through the layers of your being, and it does not transform the quality of your being. Understanding purifies. Observation leads to understanding if I am not attached to my weaknesses. People love their weaknesses: people are attached to their defects, their shortcomings. They have lived with them for such a long time that they like to justify, to explain, to defend. Unless you are attached to a habit, the habit does not last.

Observation opens the way to understanding when one is not attached to one's own image or to one's shortcomings or defects, whatever they may be. So it purifies, it cleanses. All the images that one has constructed about oneself break down completely. And understanding collects all these pieces and throws them away. They are unnecessary. The image-making business has no room in the life of a person who lives by understanding and not by knowledge. So he collects whatever broken pieces of the images he has constructed of himself in his life and puts them away: he doesn't make a bonfire and invite other people to see it. He does it quietly. This is renunciation: not having a single image of oneself. That is the essence of renunciation, *sannyasa.*

So the understanding of the psychological structure, the patterns of psychological behavior, the conditionings, one's addiction to those patterns, all these when understood in relationships, prove in the awareness of their limitations to be very dynamic. So such a person then moves in relationships in humility and in receptivity, eager to learn from the challenges of daily life unfolding itself through relationships. Learning from the challenges is the inhaling of life, and unfolding oneself as one is, through relationships, is the exhaling of life. A person who knows how to inhale and to exhale is fresh. Isn't that so? You know the art and science of inhaling and exhaling. When you are exhaling the breath, the whole of the breath that you have taken in and that entered the different parts of the body gets exhaled, so that the carbon dioxide does not get pressurized behind some organ, does not get choked up behind some muscles or glands. Unless you exhale the whole of the carbon dioxide, you cannot take in the oxygen, the fresh breath, and, therefore, the blood is not oxidized and you don't feel fresh. Inhaling and exhaling have their own elements. In the exhaling of the breath, some residue of the inhaling may be left behind. Then you feel dull. Then you get heavy. But if you know how to exhale graciously, gracefully, not with a jerk, smoothly, then the inhaling also has a joy.

So learning through challenges has new joy. When you unfold yourself totally and completely in each relationship, then speech becomes an extension of the inner silence and relationships become extensions of the inner is-ness of your life. Then the complexity of life comes to you, through your alertness and sensitivity, as a challenge. Difficulties and obstacles, unexpected, unanticipated, feel like love letters written to you by God, but it takes time to read those letters, to decipher those letters. So it becomes fun to live. There is pain bringing tears to your eyes, and you don't resist the tears, trying to choke them back with some religious precept or some moral injunction. Those tears have their own beauty. It is not only the smile that is beautiful, the tears also are beautiful, when they are not borrowed, when they are not imposed: they are born of your heart, born of the soil of your heart. So you resist neither the smile nor the tears, you do not run away from the joy and do not turn your back on the sorrow, knowing that this duality has been there for as long as human beings have inhabited this globe.

The duality, the variety, and the complexity of life is the organic nature of life. When you see that you live through all these, then you walk through the corridor of duality peacefully, serenely, and joyously, living each moment passionately, because you know that this moment is not going to be repeated. Eternity is condensed in this moment. So you meet each moment, meet each person, and meet each challenge with all the sensitivity, intelligence, and alertness at your command and live through that moment, commune with that moment, so totally, so thoroughly, that there is no desire to look back at it. When the next challenge comes before you, visited by pleasure, visited by pain, visited by prestige, or visited by humiliation, you live with that. So speech does not damage the silence, relationships do not damage the solitude, and the pleasures and the pains that are inevitable for human beings do not mutilate your joy.

CHAPTER ELEVEN

Guide, Teacher, Master, or Guru

Mount Abu; July 24, 1973

When one gets interested in the metaphysical or spiritual aspect of life, one inevitably turns toward the East, toward India, China before 1949, Japan, Tibet, Southeast Asian countries, and so on. Organized religions are not of much use to the individual who has an urge to understand the source of life and the nature of death: the meaning of living as a total action. Such a person is interested in discovering for himself the essence of love, the vehement fountain of joy inside, within himself and around himself. He turns to Asian literature and he turns to the Upanishads, the Vedas, which are not the monopoly of the Hindus. Hinduism as a religion, as it has developed and as it exists in India today, has betrayed the Vedas, has betrayed the Upanishads. The Vedas and the Upanishads, whether they were written in the Himalayan region of India or across the Himalayan ranges in Pamirs, the area of Tibet, or in Norway—a group of Indian scholars has been saying that the Vedas were written in the Arctic zone and not in the Himalayas—have nothing whatsoever to do with mythology or organized Hindu religion. In the same way, there are ancient books written in the Tibetan language, dealing with the nature of life, living, birth, death, and so on, which have nothing to do with Buddhism. Buddhism is a later development. So we find that today all the world over, those who get interested in the spiritual inquiry, psychologically and psychically, turn toward Asian countries, to their literature, their way of living, their traditions, and so on. It has been more than two centuries since the German people got interested in Indian philosophy and bought very precious manuscripts, especially the Vedas, from South Indian people. Then followed the French. India was a slave country, and so people sold the ancient manuscripts for hundreds or perhaps thousands of rupees.

So this inclination and this bias toward the Indian, the Tibetan, and the Chinese approach to life is perhaps a few centuries old. Certain words from the Sanskrit, the Tibetan, the Chinese, or the Japanese language have been adopted by the Western languages, including English. *Guru* happens to be one such word, which, unfortunately, is translated into English as "master." I wonder if the word *master* is suitable at all to convey the nuances, the subtle shades of meaning, contained in the word *guru,* coming from the Sanskrit language. The word *sisya* has been translated as "disciple." In fact, the latest meaning of the word *disciple* is "someone who voluntarily disciplines himself or herself." To discipline yourself is to educate yourself or to get educated by others. So as one travels from continent to continent, across the oceans, one meets young people at the universities or living in communes, groups engaged in cultural, religious, or spiritual revolutions. They ask me, "Do you think that you need a guru for meditation, for human transformation, for psychological mutation? Can you do it without a guru?" These questions presume that the questioner understands the meaning of the word *guru,* but I question this presumption.

A guide, a teacher, a master, and a guru: these are four different categories. They are absolutely different from one another. When you visit a country different from your own, the use of the words *foreign* and *foreigner* stinks. That is why one does not like to use them. Is there a foreign country? What do you mean by "a foreign country" or "a foreigner"? So it is a different country from your own. When you visit it, the government of that country, the Department of Tourism, arranges in different cities to take you around. The guide has to study a lot. He has to learn how to guide a person coming to that land, in a particular duration of time, about a particular aspect of city life, sharing historical, social, economic, political, cultural, and religious information about that city and that country. So you have to learn how to guide. You travel with the guide or the guide travels with you in space and in time, showing you what you want to see, showing you something that exists and that has existed and that has been described, has been defined. So there are things that are material and tangible, that have associations—historical, sociological, political, and cultural—and he has all that information and you do not. So first, he provides you with information, and second, the guide and the traveler wander together. They wander together, they go around together, and he points out the scenery, the object, the castle, the palace, the lake, and so on. He points it out and gives you the information. That is the only thing that he has to do. Whether he is interested in those objects, whether he has any love for the objects that he points out to you, is immaterial; whether he has it or does not makes no difference. So the object seen and the places visited have no relationship with the life of the traveler or the guide. They have nothing whatsoever to do with the personal life of the traveler or the personal life of the guide. It is only an inquiry or a psychological interest. I call it curiosity because it lasts a few days. It is like a sensation. I visit this country today and I see the Delwara temple, the Taj Mahal, and Gopuram. Tomorrow I visit Australia. Then I will be interested in other objects and other places. So there is a kind of intellectual curiosity, which is a healthy feeling in human life. It is a kind of psychological curiosity, which takes you around the world, but what you see and what you are told have no relationship with your personal life. You are what you were. After visiting twenty countries, you can be just the same. You are more informed, but the quality of your life, the texture of your relationships, and your way of behaving may not change. You may have gained a kind of superficial polish: you may know some words of this language, some words of that language, some information about this way of living and that way of living, and a kind of sophistication, outward, external, but inside, you remain the same.

We proceed to the second word, *teacher*. A teacher is someone who teaches out of experience. I am not referring to teachers in connection with schools or colleges who give information about certain textbooks and reference books. If the teachers present in this company would forgive me, I would say, there are no teachers today: there are information disseminators, they disseminate information, they pass on information, some in a crude way, some in an interesting way, some in a skillful way, some in an efficient way, and so on. A teacher is someone who teaches out of experience: he does not give mere information. "Truth is the nectar of life" is said in half a dozen languages. Still, he goes on telling lies three-fourths of his life. But he lives. If he has to say, "Truth is the nectar of life," he should taste of it first. So when the expression is born of his life and not of books, he is a teacher. Communications born of books can carry one through examinations, but not through life. A teacher is one who communicates out of personal experience to someone who is interested in learning that.

You can acquire information from a tape recorder or from a computer; and acquisition of information is not learning, acquisition of information or dissemination of information does not amount to education. There is no life in it. There are many things that one would like to communicate this quiet afternoon as the days of departure of my young friends are coming nearer. One would like to dive deeper and deeper into the subject at hand. A teacher is communicating out of his personal experience to someone who is eager to learn. That is to say, that which is being taught has a personal relationship with the life of both the learner, the student, the pupil, and the teacher. The teacher has no monopoly over the pupil, and the pupil has no sense of ownership or possession over the teacher. In the ninth grade, I have one teacher for history or civics or geography. When I go to the tenth grade, I have a different teacher. I attend the university and I have different teachers and I go meeting one teacher after another. A teacher meets one batch of students after another, like fresh waters flowing into the bed of a river; the waters are fresh. In the same way, in the lives of teachers and students, or pupils, there are fresh waters flowing all the time, going out to meet the sea, the ocean of life, actual life. So here the relationship is not limited to intellectual curiosity. That which is being learned, heard, or communicated has a personal relationship with the life of the person and yet there is no sense of ownership or possession: there is no "my student" or "my teacher." There is a sense of belonging, as you have in a family if it is a healthy family. You belong to one another just as there is a sense of belonging to one another in friendship, where you don't possess each other, and yet a sense of belonging, of affection, exists. So personal relationship—a sense of affection and belonging and communication—is born out of personal experience and out of the desire to learn.

We come to the words *master* and *disciple*. We will come to the word *guru* afterward. To understand the precise implications of the word *guru*, we have to find out what it is not. So we go negatively. The master is a person who communicates out of his personal experiences and discovery, but feels a sense of authority about what he is communicating, about what he is teaching. He feels that his personal discovery has something unique about it. And he considers the way he arrived at that as something special, extraordinary, but it may have been just a way: a pathless way. It might have been that he stumbled across that pathless way and he arrived at that understanding, at that freedom, that peace. But then the conditionings in which he was brought up, the peculiarities of those conditionings, the landmarks that he has come across in his inward voyage—all that he looks upon as something that can be universalized, that is capable of universal application, that is superior to other ways of inward voyages or explorations. So he feels a sense of authority over it, and when a student, or pupil, comes to him, he says, "I have this technique, this technique leads to these results for physical, for mental, for cerebral development, for specialization in certain talents and capacities, and for the development of powers: physical, psychophysical, psychological, and psychic!" So he feels a sense of authority and he feels that he can teach, provided the student is loyal to him, has faith in him, sticks to him, commits himself to the way, if not to his person. So the master accepting the disciple, the disciple accepting the master, the language changes. In teacher–student relationships, it is not so. But here on the one hand, it is the sense of authority, and on the other hand, on the part of the student, or the pupil, who comes to learn, there is the acceptance of that authority. Here it is the feeling of authority, there it is an acceptance of authority. On the part of the master, there is the conviction that his way is the only way, that his way can be taught, and that his way demands faith and loyalty and sticking it out with the master; the student feels, *I have to accept the authority of the technique, the method, and I have to have faith.* By faith, he means, *I should not question anything, I should not doubt anything.* So the imposition of authority, on the one hand, is not physical authority but psychological authority. It is imposing psychological authority in the name of liberation, freedom, meditation, *samadhi,* satori, or whatever it is, on the one hand, and on the other hand, the acceptance of authority, the willingness to conform, and the willingness to follow that authority.

So there is the sense of ownership and possession on both sides: my master and my disciple. That is how sects are born, and you have plenty of them in this country, and you have plenty of them even in Buddhism. A sectarian, dogmatic approach offers techniques and methods, formulas and blueprints, which are relevant and useful in the field of physical and mental structures. On the mental path, I include the occult and the transcendental. Techniques and methods may be useful. But this relationship invariably has led to dogmatic, sectarian, narrow approaches and competition and jealousy among those who teach or follow different ways, methods, and techniques. And the teacher's very human mind wants to propagate the teaching; his ambition leads him to construct an organization or an institution so that the teachings become permanent and are carried on from generation to generation. So a sense of authority, a desire for continuity, a sense of ownership and possession, an acceptance of authority, and universal conformity are present, and a surrender of individual freedom and initiative takes place. And what does one get in exchange? One gets in exchange some powers and some experiences: sensual, nonsensual, extrasensory, occult, or transcendental; clairaudience, clairvoyance, reading the thoughts of other people, or the capacity to materialize objects at will. Anybody who studies alchemy can acquire the power to change copper into gold or transform inner chemical conditions suddenly, abruptly, with the help of psychogenetic chemicals, ancient or modern.

All this can take place, but whatever is experienced in life has a center that takes place in time and space. In the end, having an experience implies that there is an event that takes place. And you recognize it in terms of the known, the experienced, individual or collective. An event gets converted into an experience. The moment that you are referring back to the past, your own or that of the whole human race, and you identify it, categorize it, and evaluate it, it becomes an experience. The emotional content of such an identification, recognition, and evaluation is what we call experience. So the disciple remains the disciple all through his life and the master remains the master all through his life: it is a full-time occupation.

The word *student* has a different implication altogether. Literally, it implies a state of the whole being, a state of the whole being of the person, which has no center in the individuality, which has no center at any level of his activity, in any sphere of his activity, no center, and, therefore, no circumference, no frontiers, no periphery. Not academically, not theoretically, but in all the expressions of his life, at all the layers of his being, at all the levels of consciousness, in all the fields of activity, there is no center, no me, no I, no ego, no self. It is a state of life in which assertions become impossible; there can be only communication. There is no feeling that he can teach others a technique, a method, or a formula or give others a blueprint that can protect them.

All those feelings imply a center. Unless you are conscious of your own state, you don't feel that you are capable of doing this or that. You need a feeling of self-consciousness. In order to be a master, you have to limit yourself at the psychical level, you have to come back to the center and live in the center, create a circumference around you of a terminology, of a method, of a technique, and of a sense of ownership that takes you away from being someone who lives at all the levels in all the fields, without a center and who moves into relationships without a center. How can he have a sense of authority, how can he ever claim, "Come here, I shall teach you, as the master I can initiate you and you are my disciple now." The master and disciple relationship cannot come into existence in relation to a person who, though he has a personal form, has the content in that personal form that is nonpersonal, that is not even universal, but multiversal. It is just like a bubble that contains nothing but water as the form. I could call that form merely an optical illusion, because it is all water. In the same way, the personal or the individual form of the body remains and the form of the word remains when verbal communication is gone through. But the content of a gesture, of a movement, of a word, of an action, is always universal, nonpersonal, not impersonal. The dichotomy between personal and impersonal should be left to the scholars, the philosophers, the academicians. It is neither personal nor impersonal: it is nonpersonal. That is to say, it is personal in outward form and universal in content. So he is an individual, he is a person who lives, who is capable of vibrating with life and nothing more.

That life has no direction, no purpose, no sense of mission that it must be done, that this is my ambition, that this is my work. He lives and those of us who have been together this month, communicating with one another, being together, whether for silence or for talks, are aware by now that to live is not very easy, to live is to move freely without any reservation, without any inhibition, in all the elements of spontaneity, with all the fearlessness of humility, to move with the movement of life, and to go through the challenges of life without friction. When you meet a challenge and that meeting leads to a friction within you, something is missing. If you go through a relationship without friction within you, but with friction outside you, a disharmony, a disorder outside, then something is missing. A note of music born out of the silence of the heart brings the unmanifest sounds into the world of manifestation harmoniously and goes back into the unmanifest without causing friction. When the note is not precise, it causes friction, first in the vocal chords of the musician himself and then in other chords, it causes a kind of disharmony even in the space through which it travels. So the guru is a person, a state of life in flesh and bone that has no center and no circumference. He belongs either to all or he belongs to none. He has nothing to teach. Communication and sharing is another thing. Communication never leads to a static relationship. Through communication, you share and both parties are free to live their lives. There may be mutual affection and there may be mutual respect, but even the sense of belonging is not there. What about the sense of ownership or possession? It cannot be there. There can be no static relationship with such a person.

In the same way, one would like to turn to the word *sisya*. *Guru* and *sisya:* these words have become very popular in all countries. *Sisya*—the word translated into English is *disciple*—indicates a state of consciousness, vibrating with an urge to learn, to find out, to discover truth. It is a first-hand personal discovery. An inquirer is a learner, not an acquirer, someone who is concerned with the acquisition of knowledge, information, experiences, or powers with whatever motive. Someone who is interested in acquisition wants to acquire these things, wants to store them in memory as his or her own. But why do you want to capture it as your own experience? Can you ever capture the fresh air in your fist and say, *This is my air, this is my light?* Light cannot be imprisoned in your fist. If you see a little light, if you hear some sound, if you perceive a little truth, if you have a glimpse of reality, that reality itself does not interest you; but having seen that reality becomes a terrific issue and your mind converts it into a precious experience, to be stored in memory, to be proud of, to be vain about, and then you are more interested in telling people how you feel about the experience than actually being in immediate contact with that reality. You are experiencing, ruminating over the experience, talking about it, feeling important, and feeling superior to others due to that experience. An acquirer cannot sustain the humility to learn, because acquisition is motivated by ambition. Truth cannot be acquired; love, beauty, peace, and joy cannot be acquired; they cannot be bought even with the currency of occult, transcendental experiences; they cannot be bought, purchased. You cannot bribe, bribery does not work there. It works with masters. You bribe more and you learn more than the other students. You learn the technique because it is something physical, something mental, you repeat certain types of practice. You will see that and respect certain concrete factors and you are after that. So you want more secrets. Acquisition does not sustain the humility to learn the pliability, the subtleness, of the whole being. So a sisya is a person who is out to find out, to discover, not to acquire. And once there is no temptation to acquire personal experiences, nobody in the world can enrich you, and to sustain the state of inquiry is as beautiful as to live in the state of life without a center and without a circumference.

To be in the state of a sisya or a guru is extremely difficult. An inquiry is born in the heart that prompts us to find what death is, what life is, what truth is, what peace is, and where the source of joy is. When such an inquiry is born in the life of a person, let him feel that as priceless, because it is the inquiry that is going to blossom into understanding. The state of understanding and the state of inquiry: they are not two different entities, and the fact that the inquiry is born is a great event in life, sacred and holy. If the inquiry is to find out, to discover, to understand, to learn at whatever cost it may be, it is a great event in life. That inquiry should be allowed to permeate the whole being, to permeate the whole life. Please do not restrict it by saying it is only an academic issue of life. Liberation, the state of meditation, nirvana, or satori are not academic theories: they are different names given to the is-ness, or to-be-ness, of life. So when an inquirer does not limit his inquiry to the intellectual level, he has the fearlessness to correlate it with his whole life. It is not only the mind that has to be sensitive, not only the brain that has to be sensitive: the body has to be sensitive also. The way that I earn my livelihood, the way that I live, and the way that I meet people: all the relationships at all the levels and layers of my being have to be set in time.

When the waters of inquiry are sprinkled, you get a fresh approach to your whole life. If I am not truthful in my daily relationships, why am I not? If I want to trace the source of peace, let me find out why I feel disturbed in my daily relationships. Where are the places where I get annoyed, irritated; what part gets disturbed, what damages the joy? So one begins to examine. The flame of inquiry burns brightly in your heart, and everything is done in the light of that flame. So don't say, *Oh, this is only for one hour a day,* when you attend somebody's talk or lecture. That has nothing to do with the whole way of living, and inquiry is the whole way of living. It is not a mental activity, it is a way of life.

When an inquirer works fearlessly, he relates his inquiry to the whole of his life, without compromise, without justification, and without self-defense. For example, a person who is eager to understand the truth of life would not indulge in untruth intentionally, callously, absentmindedly, or casually. He wants to understand the truth of life, so how could he utter an untruth? Because that untruth, that lie, that exaggeration, that overstatement, that understatement, would pollute his nervous system. To utter a lie is to inject poison into your own body, physical and mental. For example, if I want to find out and understand the nature of peace, why would I cause irritation, annoyance, in the lives of other people? So your whole behavior changes without your conscious effort to change it.

It is only the inquiry that helps you through your negative approach. Instead of attacking peace and joy forcibly, aggressively, you see the cause of your disturbance and it gets eliminated. Once the illusion that truth or freedom is something to be acquired takes hold, once the mind is caught in the illusion that spirituality is something to be acquired, this negative approach comes to a person very easily. So when a person relates the inquiry to his total life or, rather, relates his whole way of living to that inquiry, then a very significant change becomes noticeable.

I run the risk of being misunderstood, but I would like to say that miracles happen to begin in the life of an inquirer. Wherever he cannot understand, wherever his way gets blocked in the inquiry, life brings across his path someone who by some chance words or through communication or through gesture or relationship throws a flood of light at that point where he was blocked. Either life takes him to the individual where there is clarity, where there is understanding, where there is freedom and life without a center or circumference, or the individual who understands gets drawn physically, geographically, toward the inquirer. It seems to me that the inquirer's way of life brings together the inquirer and the person who understands without their conscious efforts to be together.

A talk, a dialogue, a conversation, the ways of condemnation by others, and suddenly the path, the avenue, opens up. An inquirer never has to hunt for a guru. Just as the law of gravity enables you to walk upon this

Earth, the solidarity of the Earth also enables you to walk upon it. And just as the law of causality, time, and sequence enables you to think and to communicate, there is a law of love in the universe, and the relationship between an inquirer and a person who understands takes place for a fraction of a second, in the same way that an unlit candle gets lit over the candle that is already lit. They meet and that meeting results in the unlit candle getting lit.

In the same way, thrown together by life, the inquirer and the understander meet. Neither has reservations or any ambition to give or to take. But being together results in an inquiry, exploring into understanding. And mind you, to live in the state of consciousness where there is no center or circumference is a tremendous thing. The intensity with which such a person lives, the vitality, the passion with which his whole nervous system vibrates, the emanation of peace and joy, the resonance of peace and love, is a tremendous thing. So when an inquirer is open, every time receptivity and humility will come, because he has not come to acquire it. There is nothing to limit his inquiry. Any acquisition conditions the inquiry and limits it. There is nothing in the life of an inquirer to narrow the inquiry down, to limit it. So there is a freshness there. The receptivity, the humility, has a tremendous freshness. So that which emanates from the person and gets transferred to the inquirer due to his openness and receptivity, without either of the two making any conscious effort, is something noncerebral, nonpsychological. They may never live together in life. There is no one to claim, *This is my guru* and *This is my sisya*. The meeting has taken place. It is an event: that is all. It is very simple. It is an event in their lives, and both get enriched.

A person who lives in the state of freedom and liberation is infinitely enriched in his joy when he comes across a person bubbling with inquiry or with an energy geared toward exploration. To come across such a genuine inquiry sends him into raptures of ecstasy. The sheer intensity of the joy of that person affects the inquiry. Nothing is taken, nothing is done. There is nothing to be done. All doing is from the center, the ego, the self, the me. Both lives are enriched and they go their own way. They may meet; they may not meet. They may be together; they may not be together. So the meeting is always for a moment and, you know, eternity lives only in the moment. A moment is condensed eternity. I want to communicate to my young friends that in spiritual life and where there is a genuine inquiry, the first step is the last. To let the inquiry be, not to suffocate it, and to correlate your life with that inquiry: that urge is the first and the last step. The rest is taken care of by life itself.

CHAPTER TWELVE

Living Together

International Youth Talk
Mount Abu; July 26, 1973

It always baffles a non-Indian coming to India with a spiritual inquiry to find an innumerable variety of paths and ways propounded authentically by individuals who specialize in those ways, methods, techniques, and paths. I would like such individuals to see the fact that India covers a vast area territorially, and has been a cradle of civilization for many races and many religions. If you travel around the Himalayan belt, the Himalayan region, including the area of Azad Kashmir, which has been under Pakistan, the valley of Jammu and Kashmir, which has been under the Indian government, Ladakh, Nepal, the northern parts of the United Provinces, Bihar, Assam—if you take the whole Himalayan region, you will come across people belonging to the Mongolian and Aryan races coming together and a mixed race coming out of that, the Aryan and the Dravidian, the natives of India and ancient India, coming together and a new mixture coming out of the union of the two races. So this whole region has Indo-Mongolian people living at the foot of the Himalayas, from a height of 4,000 feet above sea level up to 16,000 or 17,000 feet in the Himalayas.

There are hundreds of thousands of people speaking different languages that are deeply influenced by the Tibetan language and the Chinese language. And in the eastern part of Assam, the northeastern part of Assam, the language shows a little influence even of the Japanese language. So they have their own dialects. The Hindi that they speak would not be understood by the Hindi-speaking people in Punjab or U.P. [Uttar

Pradesh] or Rajasthan or other parts of India. Their sculpture is different; the way they live and their diet are also different. These people have had communication and trade with the people in Tibet and China for thousands of years. So the Tibetan approach, the Buddhist approach, not only to physical and social life, but also to religious and spiritual life, is found in these areas. They may talk of Hinduism, but the practices there, especially of tantra, are very deeply affected by the Buddhists and the Tibetans together.

You come down to the Gangetic area, the area of the five rivers in Punjab. The name Punjab means "five rivers." *Abu* (Sanskrit, "ap") is a Persian word for "water." *Panch* is a Sanskrit word for "five." Punjab is a land with five sources of water, five rivers: the Ravi, the Sutlej, the Beas, the Chenab, and the Jhelum. You come to that area and then you come to the whole of U.P. and Central Provinces, and you find the Gangetic area, the river Ganges, the river Jamuna, and their tributaries going toward the east. This area has been attacked by Mughals, by Muslims, by people from the Middle East, sometimes people from China, and sometimes people from Ubekistan, Afghanistan, and Kabul. So this area has always been full of political conflicts, turmoil, the unsteadiness of civic and economic life. The practices that exist here—religious practices and cultural practices, as well as practices in mental paths of inquiry—are affected mostly by the cultures of Kabul, Persia, and Iran, and very little by Tibet or Buddhism; there is a mixture of native Indian practices, Aryan practices, and ancient Muslim practices of mysticism, of the master–disciple relationship, of medicine, of certain words being chanted, and of certain graphs and charts being carved into metal, such as copper, silver, gold, and given to you as a charm to wear as a pendant on your necklace or on your arm. So the use of sound vibrations, too, affects the graph and the chart along with the particular kind of metal.

The science of alchemy comes from Persia; some aspects of this science come from Tibet, some from Persia, and some from Afghanistan. It did not originate in India. It was taken up by the Indians later on, and it was developed very meticulously and it has flourished a lot. Thus in the religious practices and the mental practices, you will find chanting of names, dancing, music, and drums. Drugs have also come from the Middle East, the northeast, and Tibet. Opium came from China, and hashish mainly from the Middle East, but also from the southeast. So drugs were used by ascetics, the Muslims and the Hindus alike, for getting nonsensual experiences and for expanding their consciousness. A variety of drugs known in India came from the Middle East, and they were very popular till the seventeenth century. So the practices were developed, theorized, rationalized, codified, and crystallized due to a mixture of very many currents.

In southern parts of India, there are states such as Kerala, Tamil Nadu, Mysore, some parts of Andhra Pradesh, and the coastal area of Orissa. Tamil Nadu is on the east coast, Kerala on the west, and Mysore and Andhra Pradesh are sandwiched in between the two coasts. Here you find an emphasis on knowledge as well as an emphasis on *yajna*, ritualism and knowledge. You find in the southern states of India a mixture of two races: Aryan and Dravidian. North and south India are culturally and racially very different. The languages are also very different. It is extremely difficult for northerners to understand any of the southern languages and for southerners to understand any of the northern languages. They developed altogether differently.

So we find a mixture of the Aryans and the Dravidians, Dravidians being the original inhabitants of India. They spread over Ceylon and they were in Indonesia and Australia. They told me in Australia this past year that the natives of Australia claim a racial relationship with the Dravidians in India. They say that in ancient days, Australia and India were one whole continent not separated by the ocean. They go back five thousand years, and they dream of having one continent, one state, of all these natives. They look upon the Aryans, the Europeans, the British, and the Germans as foreigners: as people of a different culture. Those people would not accept even the people in north India as belonging to them. Their religious and spiritual practices are derived from either the ritualism of the organized religion or the path of knowledge given by Shankara, the expounder of Vedanta philosophy. These practices were followed because people were not literate. Somebody had to tell people what to do and how to do it. Very few people could read and write. So you have to take the spoken word as the authority and express yourself. That is how codes of conduct must have come into existence. Very precise, chiseled-out ways and patterns of behavior were given. Take a bath only at 4 o'clock in the morning, do this, sit like that, wear these clothes, hold your nose like this, look here between the eyebrows: all these things had to be told because they were not written down, and even if they were written down, the overwhelming majority of the people were illiterate, so the authority of the spoken word was a necessity.

The authority of the spoken word, as well as the authority of the person who gave the word, was a necessity. Literature about spiritual inquiries and paths in the fourteen different Indian languages is a very recent growth. Till the fifteenth century, you would find few books written about religion or spirituality in native languages. They were all in the custody of the few brahmins living in each place, in each district or state wherever the princes ruled. This was the land of princes and states. More than 650 states existed in India hardly thirty years ago, and in every state the prince would have a learned scholar; a talented musician, instrumentalist or vocalist; a scientist; and men of literature in his court. The India that you see today as one unit was created by the British after 1860.

In 1842, Lord Macaulay wrote down the constitution; the East India Company was dissolved and the Crown Imperial took over. Till then, the East India Company was ruling on behalf of the Crown of Britain. So the concept of an Indian state is a very recent growth. There were different units, different princes, and several Muslim states: Bhopal, Hyderabad, Junagadh, Rampur, and so on. They were the centers for Muslim culture and Muslim practices. In Bengal, Assam, Bhutan, and Sikkim, the princes were Mongolians, bringing with them the Mongolian culture, along with Chinese, Japanese, and Tibetan practices. The original word for the name Assam is Aham: Aham is the name of a race coming from some southern portions of Mongolia and Manchuria. They brought their practices. The Muslim states had their own and the Hindus had their own. Thus the practices developed. But only a few brought books with them. So the authority of the spoken word as well as the authority of the person was a necessity in this country for many centuries. Whether it was the path of devotion or whether it was the path of tantra, mantra, or yantra, the necessity of authority was in the situation itself, in the social, the cultural, context. Sometimes the necessity brought pleasant results, and sometimes it brought unpleasant results.

Now, apart from the authority of the spoken word of the individual, there is one good point about the Indian tradition, which you have to remember. Living together is something that the Eastern countries, especially India, have to offer the world. When you live together, you have one purpose in mind. The uniqueness of each individual contributes to the collective culture. Every individual is unique: he looks at a question in a particular way, out of his conditionings and out of his maturity or immaturity. So when inquirers come together and live together, there is an escalation of speed for each individual and they learn from one another. Thus they had ashrams. They had places where the teacher would live, and where people would come and learn from him. So ashrams had to come into existence. Today, such centers where people can come together as inquirers, as friends, have great value, because inquiry is not an intellectual game, where you listen to a talk and then you go your way and I go my way. It is not a speculation, it is not an abstract, dry, theoretical issue.

So when you live together as inquirers, say, once a year or twice every year for a few days, it becomes a thing that refreshes you, rejuvenates you. You don't feel isolated. You learn from one another and you have the humility to be exposed as you are to your friends. Your anger is exposed, your shabbiness is exposed, your untruths, your lies, are exposed, as are your habits of lethargy, sluggishness: all that is exposed to you and to others. If the coming together is for an inquiry and not for mutual criticism, if the coming together is out of friendship and affection, then without creating a dogma, without becoming sectarian, without having a group consciousness, without having something to offer to other people, you can come together and go back, just as birds come together and go back to their places. The intimacy, the friendship, the cooperation on the footing of equality, and the learning from one another: these are the four virtues that such living together has to offer. So the inquiry does not remain an intellectual game. You don't listen to a talk, discuss it, and go away. Then you discuss your diet and how you exercise, you discuss your sleep and your dreams, and so on.

That is one point that I want to convey to you, that not as master and disciple, but as friends who have taken voyages in different directions of life, we should come together to enrich one another's lives. I think that the ancient Indian way has this to offer and the challenge is very great, to come together, to live together, to learn from one another, without converting anyone into an authority and without creating a dogma, a sect, a theory, out of it.

Now, the second point that I would like to communicate to you is, supposing that I as a non-Indian come to India, I come for the first time and I am attracted to tantra. One of my friends is attracted to the temples, the Vaishnava music, the dances, and the chanting of the mantras. Another one of my friends is attracted by the Buddhist way of meditation: vipassana meditation. A fourth one is attracted to yoga. According to our emotional and intellectual idiosyncrasies in the first encounter, we get attracted and then we get influenced. Supposing this has happened. It does not matter. One person begins with hatha yoga. Another begins with silence and sits in silence for hours. A third likes to sing, and he is charmed by the chanting of mantras. He does that. What harm is there, provided everyone is sure that he does not do a thing that he does not understand?

You are attracted, say, to the chanting of mantras. Go into it: what is a mantra? What are the sound vibrations? What do they do when I chant the mantra? What do they do to me, to my body, to my brain, and to my inquiry? Go into all this thoroughly. If an inquirer does not do a thing unless he understands it, unless he understands the implications and the relationship of what he wants to do, what he feels like doing, with his total life, then he will not be misled. It is a huge, complex thing indeed. But at least let me find out what their relationship is with my whole life, whether I begin with worshiping, whether I begin with dancing, whether I begin with chanting, whether I begin with meditation, whether I begin with studying the books—Shankara's and Nagarjuna's and Ramana's and Aurobindo's and Ramakrishna's and Krishnamurti's, or the Vedas and the Upanishads—it does not matter.

If I am attracted to something, let me begin, because in my conditionings, there may be a point that will put me in contact with the whole thing. That could be the thread, but if I am not there in my totality, then I don't accept a word of authority and I do not do a thing without understanding scientifically why it is to be done. Provided there is a scientific approach, the inquirer can never be misled: he will see the utility or the futility of the thing that he is doing within a very short time. So that is one thing: never to accept a word unless I understand the meaning thereof, never to accept an activity or a way, a technique, a method, unless I understand the implications of it and its relation to my physical and psychological life. The foundation has to be so laid that I won't do a thing and I won't accept a thing, but I will experiment with it if someone tells me to do so. But I will arrive at a personal discovery of the meaning thereof. If somebody says to me, "You won't understand, but do it because I say and because it has been done like this in India," I won't accept it.

Those who are throwing away the authority of science and technology, are they going to accept the authority of traditions in India—and for what? So that is one thing.

And second, I would do something without committing my whole life to it. If somebody says, "You become my disciple and get initiated by me, that is to say, commit yourself to be my disciple for all the years to come or get initiated into this path," with all humility I will say, "How am I to bind my future? I can be with you. If you can teach me, then I will be with you. If there are certain things that I can do for you, if I can serve, if I can help you, I will do that. But should I commit myself for my whole life?" Who are we to bind our futures, to commit our futures? "No, unless you surrender yourself to me, this does not happen." But surrender can be only to the life universal, because surrender takes place, surrender is never made. So I would say with all humility, "I am not going to bind my future. I respect you. I do the things I can do for you." So one has to proceed without committing one's whole life to it, without committing one's loyalty.

If there is to be loyalty, let it be to the truth. If there is to be surrender, let it be to the life that moves through birth and death, through growth and decay, through conflict and harmony, through tension and relaxation. If there is to be surrender, it will be of the conditioned psyche unto unconditioned psyche, the limited to the unlimited, to the total life. Humility there will be in any case, because inquiry means humility incarnate in flesh and bone. So whether I go the way of so-called surrender or devotion or mantra or *jnana*—knowledge, studying books, discussing—or I go by systems of concentration, it does not matter where I begin. If the beginning becomes a problem and an issue of discussion, then it might imply that you are trying to suppress your conditionings, that you are trying to deny the conditionings, that you are trying to ignore them.

That you feel attracted to something implies that you have something akin to it in your subconscious, in your racial unconscious. It does not matter. People who say, *You must begin this way, and you must not begin that way,* are trying to control the freedom of other individuals. That is how you are tempted to criticize others, to condemn others, to deny others, to speak derogatorily about others. When someone comes and tells me, *I don't like sitting in silence, I can't sit in silence, what am I to do? Oh! I would like to sing devotional songs, then my whole being becomes quiet and peaceful within ten to fifteen minutes*. I say, okay, proceed with that. But don't tell others that they also must sing and that singing is the only path; don't create a path for others. That you can begin elsewhere is sufficient unto itself. The moment that you begin to theorize and say, *Because I feel inclined to do this, it is like this for the others, too,* that is where the dogmas and sects are born.

Someone else says, *I like to begin with hatha yoga, which means purification of the whole system as well as the breath and the blood circulation, and purity is quietening, purity quietens you, pacifies you, relaxes you, soothes you, and purity also illumines.* So he begins the way of hatha yoga. Let it be so, as each individual is unique; the way his inquiry begins will also be unique. But what he does, what he takes, does not matter. If you take only one step in life, but if that step is taken out of understanding and clarity, then that very first step results in being the last. So those who come from different countries need not be puzzled or baffled. It will be almost impossible for them to compare all the systems and to evaluate them, unless they spend five to ten years in India and go into the whole racial and cultural history of the Indian people. It is a tremendous thing.

That is what happens to those who come to study Indian music, which is a very complex system related to ayurveda, the medicinal system; related to yoga, hatha yoga; related to so many things. Music is not only music. It is so absolutely complex: the ragas and the talas; the relation to the seasons, the time of the day, the hour of the day, and the night; and the relation to human psychology, human biology, and so on. It is a very comprehensive approach that those from the East have, not only the Indians, not only the Hindus, but also the Muslims, the Chinese, the Tibetans, and so on. So they need not be baffled if they begin to compare tantra with hatha yoga, and hatha yoga with *nada* yoga, and nada yoga with *laya* yoga. If they begin to do that, they will be lost in the forest of those innumerable paths of spiritual inquiry, because there have been so many ways, so many cultures, so many languages, and so many ups and downs.

The variety came into existence due to various factors. The variety might have been a blessing in those days; these days, it is becoming a hindrance, because people are becoming narrow-minded. The approach is exclusive, the approach is of specialization, not of having a comprehensive approach. So the complexity looks like complication. Those who are interested in making a study of this complexity may sit down and make a deep study: When did tantra come into existence? How many branches of tantra are there? Does tantra begin with the physique or with the psychology or with the psyche? Where does hatha yoga begin? What is its historical development, its location in time, its location in history, and its location in the cultural stage of the people? So it is a complex affair.

We are inquirers. So if you go around the country, see different ashrams, and meet different people (of course, in youth, there is an urge to do so), then begin wherever you feel like doing so, without wasting time. When an inquiry becomes an activity for a particular duration of time, it becomes only a dry, academic theoretical game. You can play brilliantly, or you can play in a dull way. You can play in a sophisticated way, or you can play in a crude way. But it is an intellectual game. So true inquiry is not to be postponed.

About the Author

Born in India, Vimala Thakar began her spiritual search at the age of five. As a young woman, she traveled and lectured for the Land Gift Movement of Vinoba Bhave, an associate of Mahatma Gandhi. Her meetings with J. Krishnamurti, from 1956 to 1961, had a profound effect on her life. From the 1960s to the 1980s, she taught meditation retreats in thirty-five countries. She stopped traveling outside India in 1991, and now resides in Mount Abu, India, where she still meets with people from all over the world.

From the Publisher

Rodmell Press publishes books on yoga, Buddhism, and aikido. In the Bhagavad Gita it is written, "Yoga is skill in action." It is our hope that our books will help individuals develop a more skillful practice—one that brings peace to their daily lives and to the Earth.

We thank all whose support, encouragement, and practical advice sustain us in our efforts. In particular, we are grateful to Reb Anderson, B. K. S. Iyengar, and Yvonne Rand for their inspiration.

Catalog Request
Rodmell Press
(510) 841–3123, (800) 841–3123
(510) 841–3191 (fax)
rodmellprs@aol.com
www.rodmellpress.com

Trade Sales

UNITED STATES AND CANADA
SCB Distributors
(310) 532–9400, (800) 729–6423
(310) 532–7001 (fax)
info@scbdistributors.com
www.scbdistributors.com

NEW ZEALAND
Addenda
+64–9–836–7471
+64–9–836–7401 (fax)
addenda@addenda.co.nz

AUSTRALIA
Banyan Tree Book Distributors
+61–(0)–8–8363–4244
+61–(0)–8–8363–4255 (fax)
sales@banyantreebooks.com.au
www.banyantreebooks.com.au

UNITED KINGDOM/EUROPE
Wisdom Books
+44–(0)–208–553–5020
+44–(0)–208–553–5122 (fax)
sales@wisdombooks.org
www.wisdombooks.org

Foreign Language and Book Club Rights

Nancy Green Madia
Subsidiary Rights
(212) 864–0425
(212) 316–2191 (fax)
ngmrights@earthlink.net

Index

accuracy, observation and, 44

acquisition

  climbing contrasted with, 66–67

  functional life versus, 69

  inquiry versus, 88–89

  as outward activity, 67

  swimming contrasted with, 67

  as unfulfilling, 65–66

  well digging contrasted with, 66

affluence

  cultural problems of, 37

  reaction versus inquiry regarding, 37

  turning away by children of, 23–24

  as unfulfilling, 65

alchemy, 94

anger, observing, 74, 76, 77

Aryans, 93, 94, 95

ashrams, 97

attachment to habit patterns, 27–28

attention

  accuracy and, 44

  awareness growing out of, 5, 6

  as cognition, identification, recognition, and naming, 2–3

  concentration as limited form of, 1

  concentration versus, 3, 4, 11

  defined, 2

  as harmless activity, 3

  as involuntary, 2, 10, 45

  meditation versus, 9

  motive and direction not present in, 6

  movement from concentration to, 6

  as relationship with the whole, 4–5

  self-awareness and, 43–44, 48–49

  See also listening; looking

attraction to spiritual practices, 97–100

Aurobindo, 17

authority

  exploitation resulting from, 22

  freedom versus, 7

  friendship versus, 21–22

  guidance and, 21

  in master/disciple relationship, 85, 86

  of spoken word and speaker, 96

  in teacher/student relationship, 85, 86

  understanding versus, 98–99

awareness

  absence in meditation, 46

  attention growing into, 5, 6

  being aware of, 11–12

  breathing and, 41, 45

  field of the known and, 41–42

  happenings in, 16, 18

  "I" consciousness and, 46

  as individual movement, 11, 12

  looking versus seeing and, 4

marriage of individual and universal consciousness in, 15–16

meditation versus, 5–6, 11, 31–32

movement in, 5, 12, 15, 29–30, 31–32

of nonduality, 32

as not ego-centered, 29

requirements for, 30

silence versus, 17, 18

as state of the ego, 18

time and space and, 17

of the totality, 11–12

as unconditioned, 30

See also self-awareness

Bhave, Vinoba, 66

bodily functions

breathing, 41, 45, 78–79

during meditation, 45–47

"I" consciousness unnecessary for, 46

relationship to, 55–56

universality in humans, 55

bondage

conditioning and, 53–54

naming and identifying as free of, 3

brain

cultivated, as our inheritance, 2

as invisible sense organ, 9

working with, rather than denying, 6

See also mind

breathing

art and science of, 78–79

awareness and, 41, 45

Buddhism, 81

cerebral activity. See thinking or feeling

chakras, 77

chanting, 98

civilization. See culture and civilization

cloth, as meditation seat, 50

cognition

attention as, 2–3

culture and civilization and, 10

movement of, 10

See also thinking or feeling

collective, intelligence as beyond, 15

commitment to spiritual practices, 99

comparing and evaluating

ambition and, 69

attention versus concentration and, 4

conditioning, 53

divinity as free of, 1

living together prevented by, 68

recognition growing into, 71

self compared with others, 63–64, 68

universality of, 56

concentration

absence in meditation, 33

as activity in relation to the known, 1

attention versus, 3, 4, 11

defined, 1

as limited attention, 1

movement to attention from, 6

as relationship with the particular, 4–5

resistance in, 3, 11

conditioning

attraction to spiritual practices and, 98

bondage and, 53–54

content of consciousness as, 51–52

by experiencing, 32

fashionable use of the term, 52
simplicity in relationship to,
    52–54, 67, 68
utility of, 52
consciousness
    abeyance of, 44
    awareness as marriage of individ-
        ual and universal, 15–16
    as energy or matter, 19
    See also self-awareness
culture and civilization
    activity regulated by, 10
    inquiry suppressed by, 39–40
    naming and, 10
    victimization by speed of, 38–39

deerskin, traditional yogic use of,
    51
direction
    attention as without, 6
    as limit of concentration, 1
disciple
    defined, 82
    as full-time occupation, 86
    personal center needed for, 86, 87
    "sisya" translated as, 82
    See also sisya
discipline
    defined, 82
    order versus, 26–27
discussion
    dogmatism absent from, 36
    as participatory inquiry, 35
distraction, resistance as prerequisite
    for, 3
disturbance, resistance as prerequi-
    site for, 3
divinity
    illusion of finding with the mind,
        59–60
    as unknown, 1, 17–18

dogmatism
    absence from discussion, 36
    in master/disciple relationship,
        85–86
Dravidians, 93, 95–96
drugs, 94–95
duality
    absence in meditation, 49–50
    as the nature of life, 79

Eastern spirituality, turning toward,
    81–82
eating, meditation and, 45–47
ego
    attention versus concentration
        and, 11
    awareness as not ego-centered, 29
    awareness as state of, 18
    as center of thinking or experi-
        encing, 29
    See also "I" consciousness; self-
        awareness
energy
    consciousness as, 19
    intelligence as movement of
        unconditioned, 15
    movement and, 28, 39
    as property of matter, 6, 9–10, 12
    unconditioned, as matter, 18
enlightenment
    liberation described in negative
        terms, 30–31
    meaning of, 67
    understanding and, 67–68
equality, as virtue of living
    together, 97
evaluating. *See* comparing and
    evaluating
exhaling of life, 78–79
experiencing
    conditioning by, 32

meditation viewed as, 29
as present viewed in terms of the
past, 30

feeling. *See* thinking or feeling
freedom
authority versus friendship and,
21–22
psychic, need for, 6–7, 22
as untouchable by the mind, 60
freshness, personal versus nonpersonal, 34
friendship
authority versus, 21–22
conditioning and, 54
as virtue of living together, 97
fulfillment
acquisition as unfulfilling, 65–66
the way to, 68
yearning for, 65
functional life. *See* bodily functions

God. *See* divinity
guidance, authority and, 21
guide, meaning of, 82–83
guru
center and circumference absent
in, 87–88
common questions about need
for, 82
inquirer and, 90–91
translation as "master," 82
See also master

happenings in awareness, 16, 18
health, importance of, 25
hearing, listening versus, 5, 45
Hinduism, 81
humility
of inquirer, 91, 99

as requirement for observation,
74–76

"I" consciousness
absence in meditation, 47
involuntary awareness of, 46
listening and, 43
unnecessary for bodily functions,
46
See also ego; self-awareness
identification
attention as, 2, 3
as harmless activity, 3
recognition and, 71
illusion of finding divinity with the
mind, 59–60
inaccuracy, observation and, 44
India
diversity of peoples and languages
in, 93–96
living together as offering of,
96–97
vastness of, 93
individual, the
as absent beyond awareness, 12
awareness as movement of, 11, 12
intelligence as beyond, 15
marriage of universal with, 15–16
solution to questions as within, 36
Indo-Mongolian people, 93
inhaling of life, 78–79
inheritance, cultivated brain as, 2
inner life
relationships as mirror of, 58, 63–64
transformation of, 63–64
inquirers
acquirers versus, 88–89
attraction to practices in, 97–98
attractiveness to liberated persons,
91

help miraculously drawn to,
90–91
humility in, 91, 99
living together as, 97
understanders and, 91
understanding of practices by,
98–99
whole life as concern of, 89–90
inquiry
acquisition versus, 88–89
avoiding postponing, 101
children's urge toward, 38–39
correlation with the whole of life,
89–90
cultural suppression of, 39–40
as first and last step, 91–92
as hidden in every heart, 37, 38, 39
importance or unimportance and,
50–51
motive and, 40–41
natural urge toward, 38, 39
negative approach of, 90
observation and, 74, 75, 77
pricelessness of, 89
reaction versus, 37
starting points for, 97–98, 99–100,
101
suffering as stimulation for, 37–38
understanding and, 89
intelligence
awareness as movement of, 5
meditation not a pursuit of, 34
as movement of unconditioned
energy, 15
vibration of, 6
intimacy, as virtue of living
together, 97
inverted concentration, resistance
as, 3
is-ness
inquiry and, 89

in meditation, 12–13, 34
relaxing in, 68–69

joy
as inexpressible, 60
man's lack of realization of, 65
in observing challenges, 79
relaxation as, 69
the way to, 68
yearning for, 65

knowledge
purification not possible through,
78
understanding versus, 60–61, 78
as unfulfilling, 65–66
known, the
awareness and, 41–42
concentration as activity in relation to, 1
divinity as beyond, 1
as domain of motive, 1
movement toward the unknown,
30
Krishnamurti
about, x
meaning of *conditioning* extended
by, 52
pointing beyond the known by, 18
Vimala Thakur's meeting with,
ix–x

Land Gift Movement, ix, x, 66
language
diversity in India, 93–94
love and joy as inexpressible by,
60
negative description of liberation,
30–31
precision and order needed in
speech, 25–26

of things, 50
words as symbols, 44
learning, as virtue of living
together, 97
liberation. *See* enlightenment
life functions. *See* bodily functions
listening
awareness growing out of, 5
hearing versus, 5, 45
self-awareness and, 41, 43–44, 45
living together
enrichment of lives from, 97
as inquirers, 97
as offering of India, 96–97
self-reconciliation and, 68
virtues of, 97
looking
awareness and, 4
observation growing out of, 71
at oneself, 4, 58, 63
seeing growing into, 71
seeing versus, 4
See also attention
love
man's lack of realization of, 65
as untouchable by language, 60
vision of state of, 65
the way to, 68
loyalty, truth as object of, 99

Macaulay, Lord, 96
mantras, 77, 98
master
authority and, 85, 86
dogmatism and, 85–86
as full-time occupation, 86
meaning of, 84–85
personal center needed for,
86, 87
translation of "guru" as, 82
See also guru

matter
consciousness as, 19
energy as property of, 6, 9–10, 12
movement as property of, 6, 12, 28
as prerequisite for movement, 31
thought as, 10
meditation
attention versus, 9
attraction of, 24
awareness absent in, 46
awareness versus, 5–6, 11, 31–32
bodily functions during, 45–47
as cessation of human consciousness, 31
duality absent in, 49–50
as globally fashionable, 32
"I" consciousness absent in, 47
is-ness in, 12–13, 34
marriage of individual and universal versus, 17
movement absent in, 12
as new dimension of life, 18–19
new experiences and, 31, 32
as nondual, 32
order as foundation for, 26–28
relaxation techniques versus, 32
self-awareness absent in, 48–50
as silence, 33–34
therapy versus, 41
thinking or feeling versus, 9
understanding of mind needed
for, 55
unmasking necessary for, 3
vibration in cloth used for, 50
viewed falsely as experiencing,
29, 34
mind
illusion of finding divinity with,
59–60
individual, as expression of universal mind, 57

investigation of, 57–61
limitations discovered in, 60
necessity of, 57
patterns of reaction in, 56
possession not true for, 56–57
pressurized behavior and, 58
transforming versus changing,
    63–64
understanding needed for medita-
    tion, 55
See also brain
motive
attention as without, 6
gap between expression, action,
    and, 61–62
inquiry and, 40–41
the known as the domain of, 1
as limit of concentration, 1
movement
absence in meditation, 12
in awareness, 5, 12, 15, 29–30,
    31–32
cerebral, 9, 10
as creation of the human mind, 28
of the global mind, 32
as indication of matter, 6
of intelligence, 15
of the known toward the
    unknown, 30
matter required for, 31
of the mind, 29
as property of matter, 6, 12, 28
vibration versus, 34
Moyer, Donald (Foreword by),
    ix–xi

naming
attention as, 2, 3
culture and civilization and, 10
as harmless activity, 3
negative approach of inquiry, 90

negative description of liberation,
    30–31
nonduality
awareness of, 32
in meditation, 50
nonpersonal freshness, 34

observation
anger and, 74, 76, 77
capacity for sustaining, 72
defined, 71–72
as dimension of life, 77
embarrassment by, 74
humility required for, 74–76
increasing duration of, 72–73
as innocent gaze, 72
inquiry and, 74, 75, 77
joy in challenges and, 79
living in the moment via, 79–80
looking growing into, 71
not reacting to the observed,
    72–73, 75, 76, 77–78
as not usually sustained, 71–72
in relationships, 73–76
self-deception as incompatible
    with, 74
in solitude, 73–74
as a way to understanding, 78
See also attention; listening; look-
    ing
occult, romance with, 37
On an Eternal Voyage, x
order
discipline versus, 26–27
as foundation of meditation,
    26–28
as prerequisite for transcendence,
    24–25
ownership
master/disciple relationship and,
    85–86

teacher/student relationship and,
84

Patanjali's Yoga Sutras, xi
peace
  man's lack of realization of, 65
  as relaxing in the is-ness of your
    life, 68–69
  vision of state of, 65
  the way to, 68
power, acquisition as unfulfilling,
  65–66
psychology, observation in relationships versus, 74–75
Punjab, 94

questions
  as blossoms from the heart, 35
  dogmatism and, 36
  important versus unimportant,
    50–51
  as sacred inquiry, 35–36
  solutions as within the individual,
    36
quietness, silence versus, 18, 33

Ramakrishna, 17
reaction
  dislike of, 74
  inquiry versus, 37
  toward rationalism, 53
  See also resistance
recognition
  attention as, 2–3
  comparing and evaluating grow-
    ing out of, 71
  identification implied by, 71
relationship
  to the body, 55–56
  to conditioning, 52–54, 67
  resistance as, 3

relationships
  art of moving through, 62–63
  gap between motive and expres-
    sion in, 62
  as mirror of inner being, 58,
    63–64
  observation in, 73–76
relaxation
  in the is-ness of life, 68–69
  as joy, 69
  meditation versus techniques for,
    32
religions, organized, 81
resistance
  attention as without, 11
  discipline versus order and, 26–27
  as inverted concentration, 3
  relationship implied by, 3
  See also reaction
romance
  with the occult, 37
  with the unknown, 17

satori. See enlightenment
seeing
  awareness and, 4
  looking growing out of, 71
  looking versus, 4
self-awareness
  absence in meditation, 48–50
  attention and, 43–44, 48–49
  listening and, 41, 43–44, 45
  meditation and, 43
  See also ego; "I" consciousness
self-deception
  clothing of motives and, 61–62
  observation as incompatible with,
    74
  understanding as remedy for, 67
self-observation. See observation
self-pity, 63–64, 75

self-reconciliation, 68
sentiment. *See* thinking or feeling
Shankara, 95
silence
  awareness versus, 17, 18
  cloth used for sitting in, 50
  meditation as, 33–34
  nonpersonal freshness of, 34
  quietness versus, 18, 33
  as unknowable by the mind, 1
sisya
  as inquirer, not acquirer, 88–89
  translation as "disciple," 82, 88
  See also disciple
sounds, attending to, 2–3
space
  awareness and, 17
  as prerequisite for movement, 31
speech. *See* language
spiritual practices
  avoiding dogmatism about,
    99–100
  commitment and, 99
  complexity in diversity of,
    100–101
  starting point based on attraction,
    97–98, 99–100
  understanding needed for, 98–99
staring, 72. *See also* observation
student, meaning of, 86–87
suffering as stimulation for inquiry,
  37–38
surrender, 99

tantras, 77
teacher, meaning of, 83–84
Thakur, Vimala
  about, ix–x, 103
  On an Eternal Voyage by, x
  presence of, x–xi
therapy, meditation versus, 41

thinking or feeling
  cerebral movement of, 9
  energy and movement of, 10
  as material, physical activity, 9
  meditation versus, 9
  thought as matter, 10
  See also cognition
time
  awareness and, 17
  as limit of concentration, 1
  as prerequisite for movement, 31
to-be-ness. *See* is-ness
totality of existence. *See* divinity
transcendence, order needed for,
  24–25
transformation of inner life, 63–64
truth
  knowing versus living, 60–61
  as proper object of loyalty, 99

understanding
  authority versus, 98–99
  as enlightening, 67–68
  inquiry and, 89
  knowledge versus, 60–61, 78
  observation as a way to, 78
  as purifying, 78
  simplicity resulting from, 69
  spiritual practices and, 98
universal, marriage of the individual with the, 15–16
unknown, the
  dichotomy with the known,
    17–18
  divinity as, 1, 17–18
  movement of the known toward,
    30
  romance with, 17
Upanishads, 81

Vedas, 81–82